# Divorcing Children

*of related interest*

**Social Work with Children and Families**
**Getting into Practice**
*Second Edition*
*Ian Butler and Gwenda Roberts*
ISBN 1 84310 108 4

**The Divorced and Separated Game**
*Yvonne Searle and Isabelle Streng*
ISBN 1 85302 334 5
*Lifegames*

**The Child's World**
**Assessing Children in Need**
*Edited by Jan Horwath*
ISBN 1 85302 957 2

**Engaging with Fathers**
**Practice Issues for Health and Social Care**
*Brigid Daniel and Julie Taylor*
ISBN 1 85302 794 4

**Effective Ways of Working with Children and their Families**
*Edited by Malcolm Hill*
ISBN 1 85302 619 0
*Research Highlights in Social Work 35*

**The Views and Experiences of Disabled Children and Their Siblings**
**A Positive Outlook**
*Clare Connors and Kirsten Stalker*
ISBN 1 84310 127 0

**Childhood Experiences of Domestic Violence**
*Caroline McGee*
ISBN 1 85302 827 4

**Making an Impact – Children and Domestic Violence**
**A Reader**
*Second Edition*
*Marianne Hester, Chris Pearson and Nicola Harwin*
ISBN 1 84310 157 2

# Divorcing Children

## Children's Experience
## of Their Parents' Divorce

*Ian Butler, Lesley Scanlan, Margaret Robinson,
Gillian Douglas and Mervyn Murch*

Jessica Kingsley Publishers
London and New York

The right of Ian Butler, Lesley Scanlan, Margaret Robinson, Gillian Douglas and Mervyn Murch to be identified as authors of this work has been asserted by them in accordance with the Copyright, Designs and Patents Act 1988.

First published in the United Kingdom in 2003
by Jessica Kingsley Publishers Ltd
116 Pentonville Road
London N1 9JB, England
and
29 West 35th Street, 10th fl.
New York, NY 10001-2299, USA

*www.jkp.com*

Library of Congress Cataloging in Publication Data
A CIP catalog record for this book is available from the Library of Congress

British Library Cataloguing in Publication Data
A CIP catalogue record for this book is available from the British Library

ISBN 1 84310 103 3

Printed and Bound in Great Britain
by Athenaeum Press, Gateshead, Tyne and Wear

# Contents

# List of Tables

# List of Figures

# *Acknowledgements*

Our thanks are due firstly to the children who took part in the research on which this book is based. Their words are the most important ones in this book. All of us have been impressed and moved by what they had to tell us. We hope others learn as much from what they had to say as we have done. We wish them the very best of luck in everything they do in the future.

We are grateful also to the parents of the children to whom we spoke. They will not be able to recognise their own child's specific contribution but it is here somewhere and we are grateful to them for allowing us into their homes and for the opportunity to meet their families.

The research reported here was funded by the Economic and Social Research Council as part of its Children 5–16 Research Programme, which was directed by Professor Alan Prout. We are grateful to our Advisory Committee: Rebecca Bailey-Harris, Gwynn Davis, Arran Poyser, Carole Kaplan, Martin Richards, Ceridwen Roberts and Sarah Tyerman for their interest and advice. We are also much indebted to the President of the Family Division, the Lord Chancellor's Department and the staff and officials of the Court Service without whose help we would never have been able to secure access to court records and thus to the children and families who became the subject of this book.

Frank Fincham substantially influenced the original research design. He was not able to stay with the team for the duration but his contribution to the project long outlasted his direct involvement with the work.

In acknowledging our several contributions as a research team, we have learned that interdisciplinary work can be fun! We recommend it.

*Introduction*

# Divorcing Children

This is a book about divorce seen through children's eyes. It is not a book about the longer-term consequences for children of their parents' divorce. Instead, this is a book about the lived experience of divorce, more or less as it happened. Using children's own accounts of how they experienced the breakdown of their parents' marriage, it shows how children are not only witnesses to, but also participants and actors in, the reconstruction of family life that follows divorce. To achieve this, the book reports the findings of a study conducted by a multi-disciplinary team of researchers who interviewed 104 children, aged 7 to 15, relatively soon after their parents had obtained a *decree nisi* of divorce. A detailed account of the research design and the process of data collection is provided in the Appendix.

It may be helpful at the outset to explain what we mean, and what children most often mean, by 'divorce'. At its simplest, a divorce is the point in time at which a couple's marriage is legally terminated and at which they are free to remarry. Taking a slightly broader approach, divorce may refer to the entire legal process, often spread out over several months, that the adults have to go through to bring about that final termination. But divorce is not just a legal procedure. Parents and children commonly refer to divorce to mean the entire experience of the break-up of the adult relationship and the consequences of that break-up. Usually, they regard the moment when one spouse leaves the family home, or announces their intention to end the marriage, as the starting-point of the whole 'divorce', and the time spent until that legal termination as 'going through' a divorce. In this book, when we refer to divorce we usually mean this broader process. Where we are instead focusing on the narrower meanings explained above we make this clear.

It was our intention to learn from children what it had been like for them to experience the ending of their parents' marriage: how they had coped with the experience, and what support (if any) had been available to them in adjusting to life immediately after divorce. As their accounts show, divorce should not be seen as something that only the adults do, which affects, but does not involve, the children in the family. Rather, divorce is a life-experience that is shared by all the family members, although *how* it is experienced will be different for each of them. After the initial crisis of breakdown in the adult relationship, usually accompanied by the separation of the parents (and thus, of one parent from the children), family life will continue, but it will have changed very profoundly – for the children every bit as much as for the adults. Emotional highs and lows, divided loyalties, feelings of rejection and powerlessness, and a need to assert some autonomous control over events, all feature in children's accounts of what it is like when parents split up. How children react to the crisis of divorce and how they adjust to the new situation that results, how they cope with, for example, the arrival of a new partner, and how they negotiate ongoing contact with a parent now living apart, will both affect and reflect the divorce experience for them and those around them.

## Why children? Why divorce?

We are only a few years on from the ending of the 'century of the child' (Key 1900). Whilst it is unarguable that the last one hundred years have met many of the ambitions that Ellen Key, the Swedish feminist and political radical who coined the term, had for it, it is indicative of how much more needs to be done that we feel compelled to offer a defence of why we set out to understand divorce from a child's point of view and to understand it as an experience rather than as a set of outcomes.

Perhaps the most straightforward reasons for wanting to examine divorce from a child's perspective are 'demographic'. As divorce has become more common in the United Kingdom, and as the divorce rate has climbed to the highest in Europe, so there has inevitably been a growth in the number of children affected by the breakdown of their parents' marriage. The rate of divorce in England and Wales rose from 2.1 per 1000 married people in 1961 to 13.5 per 1000 by 1991, although it fell back slightly as the annual number of divorces stabilised during the 1990s at between 140,000 and 160,000. Similarly, the number of children aged under 16 who have experienced divorce peaked at almost 176,000 in 1993, falling to 143,000 in 2000. But it is estimated that over a quarter, 28 per cent, of children will experience parental divorce by the time they reach the age of 16 (Office for National Statistics 2002, pp.44, 18). Such children therefore constitute a large group directly affected by an important social phenomenon and it might appear self-evident that we should gather their experiences and reflect on them.

The demographic 'facts' of divorce do not necessarily explain why we chose to ask children themselves about their experiences of divorce. Much research in this field has been carried out successfully with only indirect reference to children. For example, there are a great many studies that report on the longer-term consequences of divorce for children (see Rodgers and Pryor 1998 for a review of the evidence). We need to acknowledge too that a great deal of time and effort has been invested in law and public policy in this area, much of it predicated on claims to act in the interests of children. Chapter 1 describes in some detail just how public policy and legal practice have developed in recent years.

However, we would argue that what characterises public policy in the field of divorce and much of the research that has informed it, is the way in which both have regarded children as objects rather than subjects both in conceptual and practical terms. Quite literally, much of the focus on children and divorce has been a paternalistic one, emphasising the *protection* of children and often viewing them as essentially passive with little, if any, part to play in the often painful process of divorce (Piper 1996). This is a largely untested hypothesis. Comparatively little attention has been paid by policy-makers or researchers to the possibility that children might be viewed as participants and actors in the process, who create meaning and shape their own experience and who can provide an authoritative, illuminating and challenging account of this important social process.

The political and legislative framework that provides the context in which divorce takes place as well as the professional practices of those who work in this field are not, of course, unique in having largely excluded children from their explanatory and conceptual narratives. From our own, social constructionist point of view, we recognise that the history of public policy more widely is both a cause and an effect of wider shifts in the general understanding of what it means to be a child. It is only comparatively recently that a more inclusive paradigm, which recognises children's capacity to be significant authors of their own biographies, has been developed within the sociology of childhood. There is no particular reason to expect that an acceptance that childhood should be understood as a social artefact, varying across time and between cultures (see Archard 1993; Butler 1996; James and Prout 1997; Lee 2001), and which emphasises that children are to be understood as human *beings* rather than simply human *becomings* should have penetrated any more deeply into the Lord Chancellor's Department than any other part of Whitehall.

We commenced our research in the belief that children's experience of divorce needs to be understood and, even more importantly, respected and valued in its own right. We do not seek to privilege children's accounts of their experience of divorce, however. We do not see why either parents' or children's interests should predominate. But we do want to argue strongly that children's accounts be rendered on the same terms and weighed equally in the balance. We will make the point later (in Chapter 3) that parents and others cannot be considered an entirely reliable source of information on the child's experience of divorce (see also James and James 1999; Mitchell 1985; Moore *et al.* 1996). In this sense, children are not only relevant and competent witnesses to the process of their parent's divorce; they are also often the only *reliable* witnesses of their own experience.

We do not imagine that this point needs to be made to those whose work daily brings them into contact with children experiencing divorce or any other significant transition in their lives. However, it may need reinforcing for those who hitherto might have chosen to discount or disregard children's own accounts of their experience. Here we must allow the possibility that any resistance to recognising children as 'our unit of observation and as mediators of information' (Quartrup 1994, p.6) may be borne out of unwillingness as much as unfamiliarity. Reluctance to recognise the dislocation, loss and confusion described by children but which any one of us, at any age, might find ourselves faced with in similar circumstances, may be culturally constituted (see Aries 1960; de Mause 1976; MacFarlane 1986; Pollock 1983; Shorter 1976; Stone 1977 for example) but it must also be recognised as a powerful defence against a personal recognition of the distress caused to many children when their parents' marriage ends. There may even be a conflict of generational interests here. By not registering or acknowledging the lived experience of children in such circumstances, we might, with greater ease and less discomfort, be able to focus on what adults need or want when their relationships founder.

We do not intend to speculate further on whether this is another instance of the 'middle years conspiracy', whereby those who are older seek to maintain their privileged position in society. We would however wish to raise the possibility that the degree to which children's accounts of their experience of divorce (or any other matter) is able to influence the actions of adults is a reflection of our attitudes to what children have to tell us. It is not that we do not know what they have to say (in some instances) or could not find out. It is more that we simply do not want to hear it. We hope that this book may do something to undermine such attitudes, where they exist.

We might perhaps explain at this point why we have chosen to refer to 'child' and 'children' throughout the book rather than try to differentiate between, say, 'infants', 'young people', 'youth' etc., as is the current fashion. Partly, this is stylistic. Partly, it reflects the position in the law of England and Wales, which recognises no other category (although it does of course discriminate in terms of age and understanding – see Chapter 1). Principally, it is because, in our view, such gradations of childhood simply perpetuate the idea that it is age alone that determines the nature of childhood and the significance of what individual children have to say. For us, 'child' and 'childhood' are simply neutral descriptors of that class of citizens who have not yet reached the age of majority.

## Talking heads?

Our primary (but not our only) method of data collection was qualitative and much of this book is written in the words of children themselves. We do not pretend that we have managed to overcome the qualitative researcher's perennial dilemma of how to present findings that are 'true' to the underlying phenomena he or she is seeking to capture and to understand. If one adopts either a strict or a contextual approach (Best 1989) to one's social constructionism the relationship of the 'data' to any underlying social 'reality' remains one of interpretation and approximation. We do not intend to enter a full-blown defence of qualitative methodologies here although it might be helpful to make some of our assumptions clear.

Whether in relation to qualitative or quantitative approaches to data collection and analysis we neither assume reliability in the processes of perception, and inductive inference, nor presume that there are value-free, or completely objective means of assessing the 'accuracy' of different kinds of data. As Owen puts it, there is no 'view from nowhere' (1995, p.33). Our view is that despite efforts to construct notions of justification that are objective, value-free and neutral, all judgements of what constitutes 'truth/reality' or what is 'evident' within data, are based upon some normative presumptions and are inevitably context bound to some degree (see Butler and Pugh 2003).

Even if one accepts that 'man (sic) is the measure of all the measures that man has' (Smith 1997, p.86) we are still left having to decide what, according to Shaw (1996, p.27), 'makes a child or young person's account a good one'. Shaw suggests that children's accounts must bear some relation to our 'approximate understanding of real social conditions' (p.27), displaying what Martin Hammersley calls 'subtle realism' (Hammersley 1992). The account will need to be plausible and not 'fraught with obvious contradictions, stupidity and so forth'. Whilst this is largely a matter for the reader to judge, we believe the data reported here pass that test.

Other tests might be applied to the process of analysis. Gould (2000), for example, suggests seven standards that might be applied to the question of the adequacy of the data gathered. These include the adequacy of the description of the events, the claims for typicality, and theoretical and conceptual adequacy. The broad analytical themes that we draw from the data reflect the structure of concerns and issues that children raised with us during the 'scoping' phase of the research design (with one exception that is the subject of Chapter 7) and we believe that our reflections on the data are predicated on the data themselves. In the final analysis (as it were), it will be for the reader to decide how 'honest' our analysis and presentation of data have been.

We have chosen to identify the source of each quotation by (fictitious but consistently applied) name and age only. We have not, other than occasionally, provided biographical data on the child concerned. We have done this so as to give some (albeit limited) sense of 'location' for the data but not to provide too many 'qualifiers' on what children said to us that may be used to explain away (rather than simply explain) the point being made. The risk associated with such an approach is that the book may appear to some as little more than a series of 'talking heads'. Taken as a whole, however, it is our contention that the children's words recorded here provide a powerful and convincing chorus that adds considerably to our appreciation of the processes of divorce.

As far as the quantitative data reported in the book are concerned, these too are not to be understood as either qualifying or substantiating the qualitative data. Both sets of data offer the possibilities of triangulation and contribute independently to our understanding of what is being described.

## The structure of the book

As we have indicated, Chapter 1 sets out the context for this discussion of children's perspectives and experience of divorce by describing in some detail recent shifts in policy and practice in the field. The next six chapters report the findings of our study, broadly following the evolutionary progress of the divorce experience itself. Chapter 2 discusses how children found out that their parents were separating and divorcing. In Chapter 3, we report on how children went about telling other people about their new circumstances and what risks and benefits are involved. In Chapter 4, we discuss how children's relationships with their parents alter during the divorce process. Chapter 5 explores the residence and contact arrangements that are made after parental separation, the children's involvement in sorting these out, and the children's feelings about how they ought to work. Chapter 6 looks at the way in which children develop coping mechanisms and support strategies to help them come to terms with their parents' divorce and all of the changes that come in its wake. In Chapter 7, we look at children's experience and understandings of the legal process of divorce. In Chapter 8 we consider the implications of the children's accounts for both parents and the professionals whose task is to manage family breakdown and reformation. The Appendix contains a detailed account of the research process.

## Divorcing children?

The title of this book was chosen carefully. It was meant to suggest a number of thoughts to the reader that find echoes in the book itself. First, it is intended to imply that children get divorced as well as adults. It may even suggest that children somehow are active in the process of divorce. Second, it hints at an unwelcome degree of separation between children and those involved in the formal and informal processes that surround the ending of a marriage and, by extension, between children and those who determine public policy in this area. Third, its ambiguity reflects, we believe, the ambiguity that inhabits much of our thinking about children in contemporary Britain in general and those who become involved in divorce in particular. This book is an attempt to expose and address precisely that ambiguity.

## Chapter 1

# Children and Divorce

## Developments in Policy and Practice

### Families and family change

While marriage remains more popular in the United Kingdom than in many other European countries, it is clear that the number of marriages has been falling quite sharply since the 1970s, with the number of first marriages in 1999 less than half of those in 1970 (declining from almost 390,000 to 179,000). Marriage is happening later, if it is happening at all, with the average age of marriage for men rising from 25 to 29, and for women from 23 to 27, between 1961 and 1998. Remarriages are forming an increasing proportion of marriages, rising from one to two fifths over the same period. Marriages entered into by older spouses tend to be less likely to break down; however, remarriages are less stable than first marriages and more likely to end in divorce, so the effects of these two changes on the overall divorce rate may partly cancel each other out. Cohabitation outside marriage has become the norm before a marriage and especially before or instead of a remarriage. Births outside marriage now constitute around 40 per cent of all births, and 26 per cent of families with dependent children are headed by a lone parent, of whom two thirds are divorced or separated mothers (ONS 2002, pp.43, 42, 44, 18). It is clearly necessary to recognise from this mix of statistics that divorce itself is likely to become less significant as a marker of social change as marriage continues to decline. However, the process and experience of relationship breakdown and reformation are becoming ever more common, and many of the lessons that we can learn from divorce will be applicable to relationships outside marriage as well as those within. (Not everything is applicable – the legal process that spouses must go through to terminate their marriages does not, of course, apply to the unmarried, and that process itself has effects on the experience of disengagement.)

Considerable political attention has been paid to this picture of family change. But political concern about 'the family' and its apparently increasing tendency to disruption as suggested by these statistics largely reflects a conception of family life as based on a 'traditional family structure'. This is centred on the nuclear family created within marriage by the breadwinner father, whose primary role is to support the family economically (Collier 1995; James and Richards 1999), and the nurturing mother who takes primary responsibility for the care and upbringing of the children. However, feminist and economic imperatives have prompted attempts to encourage female employment after childbirth, and these have been met by a male and conservative reaction that seeks to involve fathers more actively in their children's lives. Both developments run counter to the traditional model of parenthood by envisaging a more equal sharing of roles between the parents. They have created pressures, both during and after marriage, which can make adherence to both the traditional or the 'new' model of parenting impossible to sustain. Where the traditional model was employed during the marriage, it may be emotionally difficult and unfair to expect the parents to embrace the 'new' model afterwards (Smart and Neale 1999). Yet it may be economically impossible to continue the traditional role of the mother post-divorce when insufficient income prevents her from remaining 'at home for the children' (Perry et al. 2000). The stresses and strains of coping with these conflicting expectations may contribute to the emotional burden of the marriage breakdown. At the political level, government may proclaim its willingness to treat different family forms equally (Home Office 1998) but underlying social and economic structures, coupled with cultural norms and political calculations, can re-create the same confusion and ambivalence experienced by individual families.

Much has been written on the emphasis on personal and individual fulfilment in 'late modern' society (Beck and Beck-Gernsheim 1995; Giddens 1991, 1992). The Giddens conception of the 'pure relationship' entered into by autonomous adults, which is constantly negotiated and renegotiated and which is inevitably fragile and prone to fracture, appears borne out by the seemingly high divorce rates in western society. As Smart and Neale (1999, pp.6–19) have pointed out, Giddens' writings fail to attach much significance to the presence of children as the products of an intimate relationship. Beck and Beck-Gernsheim, by contrast, do focus on children. But they appear to see them as objects of affection and ambition – Giddens' project of the self becoming embodied in the child who is to be shaped to the adult's perceptions and needs. Neither contribution has much to say about children's own agency and capacity as social actors. But both accounts appear confirmed by the recent growth in concern amongst politicians and policy-makers about the interests of children whose parents' marriage has broken down. Indeed, one of the most significant shifts in legal focus in recent years has been away from the adult relationship towards that between parent and child, and towards the needs, interests and finally the rights of children themselves.

## The position of the child in divorce

One explanation for the paternalistic approach towards children affected by divorce (described above) is that they are commonly viewed as suffering a pathological experience. Indeed, there is now a considerable body of research evidence suggesting that children may face detrimental outcomes from parental separation and divorce. In a thorough review of the available evidence, Rodgers and Pryor (1998) concluded that the children of separated families have about twice the probability of experiencing poor outcomes in the long term, compared to children in intact families. These outcomes include greater levels of poverty, lower educational attainment, poorer health, higher levels of behavioural problems and depressive symptoms, and higher levels of smoking, drinking, drug abuse and teenage pregnancy. The risk of suffering such outcomes is associated with parental conflict, parental distress and multiple changes in family structure.

Such findings help explain in part why divorce has come to epitomise an area of public anxiety and of uncertainty. It has been argued that the focus on the position of children in divorce is a form of projection of anxiety about the uncertainty in our own lives, and that in seeking to 'protect' children, we seek to protect ourselves (Brown and Day Sclater 1999). This insight helps us see that the child can be viewed as situated at the centre of a net of concerns and pressures regarding the family. Political and legal responses to this set of social and cultural changes have embraced conflicting agendas at varying times and even simultaneously.

## From rights to welfare to rights

Family law during the past century has experienced change of a comparable order to the social changes that it accompanied and reflected. Until the later part of the century, divorce carried a severe social stigma, which was reflected in the legal conception of divorce as justifiable only where the matrimonial fault of a guilty spouse could be established. Once such fault was proved, the guilty party could be deprived of his or her care or contact with the children. A 'guilty' wife had no 'right' to keep her children with her after divorce. As Lord Denning trenchantly observed in a case decided in 1962:

> a mother must realise that if she leaves and breaks up her home in this way she cannot as of right demand to take the children from the father.[1]

Divorce law was reformed in 1969 by the Divorce Reform Act, later consolidated by the Matrimonial Causes Act 1973, which introduced the concept of 'irretrievable breakdown' as the sole ground for divorce. This was intended to remove, or reduce, the emphasis upon the 'fault' or blame of one of the spouses as the reason for ending the marriage. However, the law retained certain forms of matrimonial 'fault' (adultery, behaviour and desertion)[2] as a basis for proving irretrievable breakdown and the first two of these remain the main routes for obtaining divorce (Lord Chancellor's Department 2002a). Nonetheless, the new political attitude towards divorce enshrined in the legislation coincided with – and no doubt also reflected – a decline in the stigma attached to divorce. Moreover, as divorce became more common throughout the 1970s and 1980s, there gradually dawned a realisation that, notwithstanding the termination of the marital relationship, the parent–child bond remained and was of value, or, as Margaret Thatcher once memorably put it, 'parenthood is for life'.

This recognition was part of an increasing emphasis upon the welfare of the child in family proceedings concerning children (O'Halloran 1999). In fact, the Guardianship of Infants Act 1925 had made the child's welfare the 'first and paramount consideration' of a court in determining any questions regarding the future upbringing of a child. But it was not until nearly fifty years later, when first case-law[3] and then legislation[4] reiterated the principle, that it really received wide public and political recognition. With welfare as the paramount, and in practice, the only, consideration that the court had to take into account, arguments referring to parental rights, particularly ones based on conduct and misconduct in the marital relationship itself, received increasingly short shrift.

A pattern gradually emerged of the day-to-day care of the child (now known, under the Children Act 1989, as 'residence') usually vesting in the mother, reflecting her continuing role as the primary care-giver. Fathers would be awarded contact (formerly referred to as access) to take place at weekends, during school holidays etc. The problem with this pattern was that it appeared to involve the mother (usually) 'winning' the care of the children, even where she might be to blame for the break-up. Although the judges were clear that issues of 'justice' were irrelevant, the result could often cause considerable anger and a sense of injustice on the part of fathers. This was reinforced by the growing calls for fathers to become more involved in their children's upbringing and not simply to provide the wherewithal for meeting the family's economic needs. One mechanism intended to address this sense of grievance was introduced by the Children Act 1989. Section 2(1) of the Act provides that where a child's parents were married to each other at the time of his birth, they shall each have parental responsibility (parental rights and duties) for the child. This parental responsibility endures throughout the child's minority, unless the child is adopted. Thus, even where it is decided that the child is to live with one parent after a divorce, the other retains his or her parental responsibility and his or her right to share in taking the major decisions about the child's upbringing. The Law Commission, which recommended this concept, considered that this would 'lower the stakes' in parental disputes over their children's futures, and reduce the 'win/lose' dimension to the outcome of court cases. But this has, to some extent, perhaps ironically, revived the notion that parents have certain rights in relation to their children, at least to attempt to forestall major decisions by the parent with day-to-day care.

In 2000, the Human Rights Act 1998, which brought the main provisions of the European Convention on Human Rights into domestic law, came into force. Article 8 of the Convention provides that everyone has the right to respect for 'his private and family life'. A number of divorced fathers have attempted – so far unsuccessfully – to use Article 8 as the basis for actions in the domestic courts to prevent a mother with care of the child from, for example, taking the child permanently to live abroad,[5] or from curtailing the father's contact with the child.[6] It was suggested in such cases that Section 1(1) of the Children Act 1989, which now provides that the child's welfare is the court's 'paramount consideration' in determining questions relating to the child's upbringing, was incompatible with Article 8, since it appears to provide that the parent's right *must* be overridden when the child's welfare so demands. The courts in England and Wales have rejected such claims, and the European Court of Human Rights has itself recognised that the child's welfare may be 'overriding'[7] in the event of such conflicts (Fortin 1999; Herring 1999).

None of this, however, takes us any closer to 'knowing' what is in a child's best interests. The welfare principle has been condemned as vague and amenable to being used as a justification for any outcome that the decision-maker prefers, be that based on possibly misunderstood evidence of a bevy of experts, 'common sense' or downright prejudice (Davis and Pearce 1999; King and Piper 1995; Reece 1996). There is a danger that broad generalisations derived from such sources become regarded as truth or wisdom about children's interests, when they may have more to do with cultural norms and political imperatives.

## The recognition of children's rights

If we cannot rely on 'welfare' to provide an objective measure for determining how children can best be cared for and supported after divorce, would an appeal to the rights of the child serve us any better? It is certainly the case that, alongside social and cultural changes in attitudes and behaviour regarding the family, there also developed perhaps the most significant achievement of the 'century of the child' – the recognition that children might themselves be regarded as citizens with their own rights.

The idea of children's rights (Archard 1993, 2001; Fortin 1998; Van Bueren 1995) is not straightforward. The whole concept has been criticised by King and Piper (1995) on the ground that rights talk is used to justify decisions that would be reached on other grounds anyway, and that to proclaim that a child has a 'right' to something says nothing about how that right is to be fulfilled. Rights talk may indeed run the risk of becoming empty rhetoric, but the virtue of rights claims are that first, they can forestall objections and need no justifications – the fact of having the right is itself the justification. Second, they reinforce the position of the rights-holder as an actor and citizen rather than as an object and dependant.

But there is a further problem concerning children's rights. How is a child, who may be unable to act for him or herself, actually to *exercise* their rights? One theory of rights argues that the existence of a right depends upon whether the rights-holder is able to choose whether to assert the right or not. An infant cannot exercise such a choice (any more than an animal can), and so it might be concluded that a child (at least below the age at which he or she can reason) *cannot* be a possessor of rights. This view has been challenged by the development of an alternative theory, based on the *interests*, rather than the *will*, of the rights-holder. In this theory, a right can exist in order to uphold the rights-bearer's *interests*, and can be enforced by another acting on behalf of the rights-bearer (MacCormick 1976). On the assumption that this approach is clearly more helpful in finding a means of establishing a basis for the concept of children's rights, we can then go on to assess what such rights might consist of. The broadest categorisation is to divide them into those relating to the child's welfare (or perhaps, their 'interests') and those pertaining to the child's autonomy (that is, the child's freedom to choose a course of action for him or herself). For example, Freeman (1983) categorises children's rights into those relating to welfare, protection, treatment as an adult would be treated, and rights against parents. Eekelaar (1986) adopts a similar model, recognising three types of rights – basic, developmental and autonomy rights.

## Children's rights in international law

An ambitious attempt to bring these rights together in international human rights law was made with the promulgation of the United Nations Convention on the Rights of the Child in 1989. The Convention, which has been ratified by virtually all states who are members of the United Nations, attempts to provide a comprehensive statement of the rights that children should enjoy, both as children, and as legal *persons*. Thus, it contains rights that are intended particularly for children (such as the right under Article 28 to primary education) as well as rights also enjoyed by adults (such as the right to freedom of conscience in Article 14). It brings together both civil and political rights (which focus on the rights-holder as a member of the polity within the state) and social and economic rights (which are concerned with redressing class and gender disadvantages). One commentator has suggested that these myriad rights can be classified as the four 'Ps' – prevention, provision, protection and participation (Van Bueren 1996). It is the right to participate – to contribute to decision -making in matters affecting the child – that is central to the discussion in this book.

Although the United Kingdom ratified the Convention in 1992, it is not part of English domestic law. This means that although the United Kingdom government must seek to abide by its provisions, the Convention cannot be directly relied upon in any legal proceedings in the courts in England and Wales. However, the courts may take it into account in their interpretation of domestic law and will seek to ensure, if possible, that such law is compatible with the Convention's terms. Nonetheless, in the event of a clear conflict between the Convention's requirements and English law, the courts must give effect to the latter and not the former.

Perhaps in part because of the lack of incorporation of the Convention into domestic law, it has so far had little real impact on the law in England and Wales. But that which has prompted most thought and raises perhaps the most important issues for the development of the law is the child's 'right to be heard' contained in Article 12. This is the precursor to any right to participate in decision-making. Article 12(1) provides that:

> States Parties shall assure to the child who is capable of forming his or her own views the right to express those views freely in all matters affecting the child, the views of the child being given due weight in accordance with the age and maturity of the child.

This provision is probably the central Article in the Convention because it is here that the conception of children as actors in their own right, rather than as the appendages of adults, finds its clearest expression. It will be seen that it imposes a general obligation on the state to find ways of enabling the child 'capable of forming his or her own views' to express these in relation to 'all matters' affecting him or her. It should be noted that the child's right is not dependent upon his or her ability to *express* views, but to *form* them. This means that even quite young children must be afforded means of communicating their views – in other words, the onus is on the state to find out what the child's views are, if necessary by finding non-adult ways of determining them. One may think here of the use of pictures rather than words to communicate information. The weight afforded to the child's views will, however, be subject to considering his or her understanding and maturity. It is obvious that it may not always be possible, still less desirable, to follow the child's wishes in all matters, but the older and more mature the child is, the more weight should be placed on his or her wishes.

## Children's rights in domestic law

The significance of the child's developing intellectual maturity and autonomy was already recognised in English domestic law before Article 12 was drafted. In *Gillick v W Norfolk and Wisbech Area Health Authority*,[8] the House of Lords held that once a child is of sufficient maturity to understand the implications of their decision, she or he is entitled to give a valid consent to medical treatment. This is regardless of parental views, and indeed, the parent has no right even to know to what the child is consenting. This idea of 'Gillick competence' has been extended to other areas of the law, such as to permit a child to be represented by their own choice of lawyer in legal proceedings.[9] It also finds expression in several provisions in the Children Act 1989, intended to focus the attention of courts and local authorities dealing with children upon what the child's own wishes and feelings are in the matter being decided.[10]

As explained above, the United Nations Convention cannot currently be directly relied upon in legal proceedings. But children, as well as adults, may seek to rely upon the rights enshrined in the European Convention on Human Rights. This means that, in the event of a dispute between the parents over, say, whether the mother should be permitted to move abroad permanently with the child and her new partner, the court is obliged to take account of the right to respect for family life protected by Article 8, which is possessed by both parents *and* the child. This requires a balancing of these different family members' rights, and no one member has a pre-emptive claim. Thus, where the court finds that preventing the move would run counter to the child's own Article 8 right to be settled in the family unit created by the mother and new partner, it cannot conclude that the father's right should prevail, even though removal may prevent him exercising it. In practice, the child's 'right' will be merged with what the court considers to be for his or her welfare, but courts are increasingly using the Article 8 right enjoyed by the child (and the other parent) as a second justification for the conclusions they reach. Moreover, the European Court also refers to the United Nations Convention on the Rights of the Child in reaching its conclusions in such cases, reinforcing the central position that the concept of *children's* rights has now taken in legal thinking about children's relationships with others (Opromolla 2001).

# The growing legal recognition of the position of children in divorce

## The welfare check

Concern for children whose parents divorce is not new. Since 1958, the person seeking the divorce (the 'petitioner') has been required to inform the court of their proposed arrangements for the care and upbringing of any dependent children of the family. Originally, the court could not (unless there were circumstances making it desirable to do so without delay) grant a decree absolute of divorce legally terminating the marriage without first declaring that the arrangements for the children's future were 'satisfactory or the best which can be devised in the circumstances, or... that it is impracticable for the party...to make any such arrangements' (Matrimonial Proceedings (Children) Act 1958, s2(1)). In the 1970s, the procedure for obtaining a divorce was radically altered; there was no longer an oral hearing of an undefended divorce petition. Instead, the decision whether to grant the divorce was to be undertaken on the basis of scrutiny by the judge of written papers only. A system of 'children's appointments' was introduced, whereby the judge interviewed the petitioner (with or without the other parent, and sometimes in the presence of a court welfare officer) to check on the proposed arrangements for the children (see Davis et al. 1983).

## The Children Act 1989

In the 1980s, the Law Commission (1988) carried out a comprehensive review of child law, resulting in the enactment of the Children Act 1989. In the context of divorce, the Act abolished the 'children's appointments' system and replaced it with scrutiny of a detailed 'statement of arrangements' filed by the petitioner and setting out their proposals for the children. The duty placed upon the divorce court was changed from requiring the court to be satisfied as to the proposed arrangements for the children, to instead obligating the court to 'consider (emphasis added)... whether it should exercise any of its powers under the Children Act 1989 with respect to [any children of the family]' (Murch et al. 1999). The assumption that lies behind this approach is that parents may be trusted, in most cases, to plan what is best for their children's futures. Further, where they are in agreement on this, it is regarded as unnecessary and potentially damaging for the state, in the guise of the court, to intervene. As the former Lord Chancellor, Lord Mackay, explained:

> The principle is that the court should not intervene…unless it is necessary. The family is best able to decide these matters, but the Children Act facilitates the intervention of the court.[11]

The 1989 Act replaced the old legal terminology of 'custody' and 'access' with new orders for 'residence' and 'contact'. The former of these is 'an order settling the arrangements to be made as to the person with whom a child is to live'. The latter is 'an order requiring the person with whom a child lives or is to live, to allow the child to visit or stay with the person named in the order, or for that person and the child otherwise to have contact with each other'(Section 8) (see Trinder *et al.* 2002). The purpose of these orders is simply to sort out the practicalities concerning the children after the parents separate, and not to confer winner or loser status on the parents. Moreover, Section 1(5) of the Act provides that courts should not make any order unless satisfied that doing so would be better for the child than making no order at all. Accordingly, where parents reach agreement on what is to happen to their children, they may be refused an order on the basis that it is unnecessary. Drawing on the research noted above regarding the damaging effects of parental conflict and on a prevailing ethos in the legal process of encouraging settlement, the courts and family lawyers promote the message that it is far better for children if their parents can reach compromises rather than go to court (Davis and Pearce 1998).

## The Family Law Act 1996

Further divorce reform was proposed during the 1990s (Law Commission 1990) and enacted in the Family Law Act 1996. The new law aimed to move divorce completely away from any basis in matrimonial fault, by providing that divorce could be obtained simply by one spouse giving notice of intent to the court and then waiting for a set period of time to elapse. It also sought to ensure that the parties appreciated the implications and consequences of going through a divorce at the outset, and to promote settlement, rather than litigation, of the issues arising from the ending of the marriage – division of property, provision of support and care for the children. Section 1 of the Act sets out general principles to which the court and any person (such as a lawyer or mediator) exercising functions connected with divorce are required to have regard. These include the following –

(c) that a marriage which has irretrievably broken down and is being brought to an end should be brought to an end:

   (i) with minimum distress to the parties and to the children affected;

   (ii) with questions dealt with in a manner designed to promote as good a continuing relationship between the parties and any children affected as is possible in the circumstances...

(d) that any risk to...any children, of violence from the other party should, so far as reasonably practicable, be removed or diminished.

The court would still be required to carry out a check on the proposed arrangements for the children, and would now be required to have particular regard to a 'checklist' of factors, including 'the wishes and feelings of the child, considered in the light of his age and understanding and the circumstances in which those wishes were expressed'. As Lord Irvine noted during debate on the Bill, this provision:

> is fully in tune with the new and increasing contemporary awareness that a child is a person in his or her own right...the divorce process must now have regard to the interests and views of the children. They will now have a right to be consulted about the proposals which the parents are making for the future in which they have a vital interest.[12]

As we show in subsequent chapters, the extent to which children are *currently* consulted by their parents, and how far they can exert an influence, in arriving at decisions concerning post-divorce arrangements, varies widely between families and reflects the abilities and willingness of both parents and children to communicate with each other over difficult and sensitive issues. Given this variation, quite how this provision could have been brought into effect remains a matter for speculation, because the government decided in 2001 not to implement these divorce reforms. A mix of both liberal and conservative values had underlain their enactment, reflecting a clash of views both within Parliament and the country at large, and satisfying neither. The Conservative government, uneasy at criticism of its new Act, and having learned its lesson from the hostile reception that greeted implementation of the new Child Support scheme in 1993, undertook to pilot-test key features of the new divorce procedure before bringing the law into force. The return of a Labour government in 1997, with a fear of upsetting the middle class who had voted for it at long last, resulted in a timid approach to family policy. It shelved divorce reform, claiming that the pilot studies demonstrated that the system set out in the 1996 Act would not deliver the hoped-for gains of more reconciliations as parties reassessed whether they truly wished to end their marriages, and of more settlements via mediation.[13]

## Children's rights, children's welfare or children's perspectives?

Notwithstanding the abandonment of the legal reforms, it is clear that children's needs and interests have over time assumed more significance in the legal process of divorce. Their recognition has also been important in developing our broader understanding of family dynamics, the psychological impact and the social implications of family break-up. But as King and Piper point out (see above), a parroted call to 'respect children's rights' tells us very little about how children's needs and interests should be taken into account either by individual families experiencing divorce, or the wider community providing services and support to such families. Appeals to 'welfare' are no clearer than claims of 'rights' in telling a court – or parents – what is best for that particular child.

Moreover, it is important not to generalise about children, assuming a homogeneous experience and response, as we demonstrate throughout later chapters. One approach to advocating a children's rights perspective has been to describe children as a 'minority rights group' like women (sic), ethnic minorities or the disabled (John 1996). But this runs a risk of conflating different children's perspectives. Our study of a particular sample of children whose parents have divorced makes it clear that different children experience the same events very differently, making it all the more vital that their individual experiences are validated and taken into account. Indeed, it is through an appreciation of children's *perspectives* that we believe the, perhaps artificial, conundrum of rights versus welfare can be resolved.

Children's position as members of communities and society is now increasingly being recognised. Yet, children have been excluded from being directly involved in the legal and formal processes when their parents divorce. This is partly because their interests may clash with those of their parents, and partly because the state has hesitated to 'interfere' in the decisions that parents make for their children and is rightly wary of constraining parents' own freedom of action in forming and rejecting intimate relationships. But since adults have more power, their views have usually prevailed, both within families and in the public sphere as well. Realisation that this state of affairs is no longer acceptable now permeates most public policy-making surrounding family life. However, it will not be sufficient in the future to instruct parents of the importance of taking their children's interests and views into account, if public policy and procedure continue to be shaped without being influenced by these.

The next six chapters represent our attempt to have the voices of children heard.

## Notes

1   *Re L (Infants)* [1962] 1 WLR 886.
2   Section 1(2)(a)(b)(c), Matrimonial Causes Act 1973.
3   *J v C* [1970] AC 668, HL.
4   Section 1(1) of the Children Act 1989 made 'welfare' the 'paramount' con-
    sideration.
5   *Payne v Payne* [2001] EWCA Civ 166, [2001] 1 FLR 1052, CA.
6   *Re L, V, M, H (Contact: Domestic Violence)* [2001] 2 FLR 334, CA.
7   *Elsholz v Germany* [2000] 2 FLR 486.
8   [1986] AC 112, HL.
9   *Re S (a minor)(independent representation)* [1993] 3 All ER 36.
10  Sections 1(1)(a), 22(4), 38(6), 43(8), 44(7).

11  HL Debs vol 568 col 1163, 25 January 1996.

12  HL Debs vol 573 col 1076, 27 June 1996.

13  Official Report col WA126, 16 January 2001.

## Chapter 2

# Finding Out

The children in our study typically experienced family breakdown and the consequent disruption to their everyday lives as a form of crisis. Whilst it is difficult to define a crisis (see Coulshed 1991; O'Hagan 1986) because of the way the word is so widely used and abused, professionals' use of the term tends to reflect Rapoport's (1970) definition, which describes a crisis as 'an upset in a steady state' (p.276). This steady state has also been referred to as homeostasis or psychological equilibrium and the crisis as a turning point where 'the individual's coping resources have been surpassed and a new approach has to be developed' (Thompson 2000, p.79). It is in this sense that the term is used here. This is not to suggest that most children's response to their parents' separation is somehow pathological in nature. As Coulshed (1991, p.40) makes clear:

> ...crises occur throughout life; we constantly make adaptive manoeuvres in order to cope and maintain our equilibrium... Crises can be perceived as a threat, a loss or a challenge encompassing danger but also opportunity for growth, especially when the situation is mastered and new methods of coping found.

In trying to understand how and why children make sense of and respond to the break-up of their family in the ways that they do and how they begin to develop more or less adaptive strategies and coping mechanisms in order to recover their psychological (and social) equilibrium, it is important to trace how an awareness of their parents' separation originates and develops for children, to understand *how* children find out that the practical and emotional infrastructure of their lives is about to change decisively.

Crisis does not mean the same as 'emergency'. Even events that are anticipated can be experienced as crises in the sense that we are using the term. Crisis is a function of one's reaction to a situation; it is not intrinsic to the situation itself. For some children, awareness that the familial *status quo* is about to alter begins in the evident conflict taking place between their parents. Often, this is recognised in the frequency and intensity with which their parents argue.

> I used to hear them arguing. They always used to shout at each other and basically scream their head off at each other. Me and my brother were sat on top of the stairs and we used to hear them shouting in the kitchen. It felt horrible. I felt that I was the only child that's parents were getting divorced. Every morning you could hear them shouting and every evening when you got back from school and it was non-stop arguing.
>
> Sioned, aged 12

> I knew what was gonna happen 'cos they argue too much.
>
> Ellie, aged 10

The majority of children seemed to have witnessed their parents arguing at some point. Some parents had made attempts to hide their arguments from their children. Nonetheless, these same children usually reported the upsetting experience of having to listen to their parents arguing while they were in another room or in bed trying to sleep.

> I was in bed trying to take my mind off it; trying to watch TV and all that. They were talking so loud I just decided to listen and listen till I heard a massive great big THUMP and that's when I started to cry. I didn't want it to happen any more.
>
> Jonathan, aged 12

A smaller number of children also witnessed incidents of violence between their parents.

> It was so vicious – me and Damian [brother] in the kitchen; we were under the table. Mum and Sam [step-father] walked into the kitchen arguing and Sam got so mad he threw plates at Mum and Mum was like

crying and screaming and I was so scared. We were sitting there for ages just shaking, crying, screaming and it was just horrible.

Ellie, aged 10

I could hear him calling her things like, 'You stupid idiot', things like that. Then my father came round and told me to go in my bedroom and he was just calling her names. In the night, he pushed her down the stairs. He used to do things like that.

Jenny, aged 8

By the time of separation, most children knew at least that all was not well between their parents and some had begun to feel that their parents' separation was inevitable. As far as being told explicitly about their parents' separation goes, it is important to note that children and adults recall this process differently. Over two thirds (70.9%) of children indicated that they had been told by one or both of their parents about their separation, with the remaining third (29.1%) reporting that they had not been told. In contrast, every parent (except one) indicated that they had either severally or jointly told their children about their separation (see Figure 2.1). Clearly, 'telling' or 'not telling' is a function of the quality of the exchange and it should not be thought that anyone is misrepresenting the communication that occurred between parents and their children. This discrepancy may be attributable in part to differential recall of events and age seems to have been an important factor. One hundred per cent of children over the age of 12 reported that they had been told, compared to only 82 per cent of children aged between 10 and 12 years. This figure drops even further for children under the age of 10 of whom only 66 per cent recall being told about their parents' separation (see Figure 2.2).

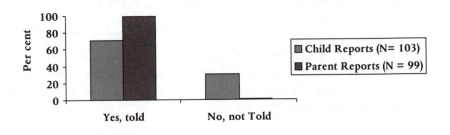

*Figure 2.1 Were children told about the divorce?*

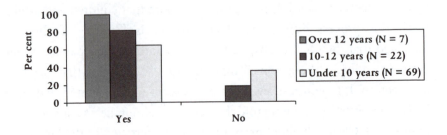

*Figure 2.2 Age at seperation and recall of being told*

Qualitative data from both parents and children highlighted another important factor that needs to be considered. Divorce was a new, uncharted and stressful experience for everyone involved and parents and children alike often reported that they had not been sure what to say or how to say it. Parents said that they did not know what was happening themselves and did not know what to tell their children. Children in turn felt that they did not know how to ask for the information they felt they needed. Both parents and children reported that they had shied away from talking about the divorce because each felt the need to protect the other. As Shaun (aged 12) put it:

> I didn't feel like, I mean, you know it's a bit depressing to ask somebody who is getting divorced about divorce, you know!

It remains the case however, that for a significant proportion of children, little by way of explanation or preparation had *effectively* been undertaken by parents, as far as children themselves were concerned. We return to the subject of communication between children and their parents below and at several other points throughout this book. In particular, we will examine how failures of communication between children and their parents not only affected how children understood what was happening in their parents' marriage and what was likely to happen to them as a result of its breakdown but also how important effective communication was in the process of relationship building and rebuilding after separation had taken place.

Where children were able to describe the ways in which their parents told them about the separation, their experience varied greatly. Most children (46.6%) believed that this *should* be a task for both parents (see Figure 2.3). According to the children, in only 12.6 per cent of cases was this the case. In fact, the largest proportion of children was told exclusively by their mothers (51.4%) (see Figure 2.4).

> Mum sat us down. I don't like our front room any more because we always go to the front room when something really bad is happening 'cos when Dad had a problem, we came to the front room. And that was upsetting. Then Mum sat us down and told us. So I don't particularly like the front room.
>
> Sophie, aged 15

The girls in the sample were more likely than the boys to report being told about their parents' separation by their mother. Eighty one per cent of girls who had been told, reported that it was their mother who told them compared to only 67 per cent of boys.

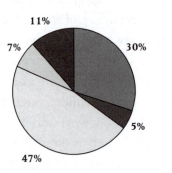
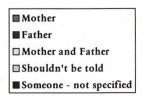

Figure 2.3 Who should tell the children about the divorce?

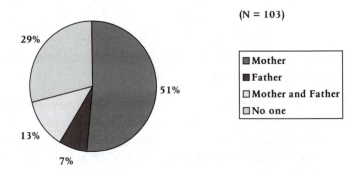

Figure 2.4 Who told the children about the divorce?

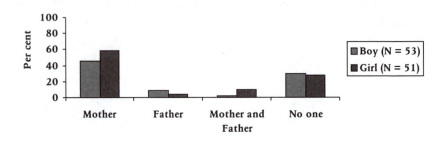

Figure 2.5 Who told the children about the divorce, shown by gender

Only 6.8 per cent (see Figure 2.4) of children were told by their fathers. This tended to occur in families where the child's mother had already left or was going to leave.

> He brought me into my room, he said that 'Me and Mum aren't getting along very well and we're always shouting at each other and so Mum's just gonna try and get a little house down the street'; because every time I was seeing them they were always arguing.

> Sioned, aged 12

Most children seemed to have particular difficulties in talking to their fathers about sensitive and emotive issues, feeling it was easier to talk to their mothers (see also Chapter 4). Over a third of children (36%) said that they absolutely refused to talk to their fathers about the divorce compared to 11 per cent who reported that they would refuse to talk to their mothers (see Figure 2.6). Half of the children we spoke to (50%) said that their fathers knew nothing or very little about their feelings about the divorce, while only 20 per cent of mothers fell into this category (see Figure 2.7). Almost two thirds of children reported that they never or seldom talked to their fathers about their feelings about the divorce (see Figure 2.8). This reluctance was apparently shared by many of the fathers who might try to avoid talking to their children about the marriage breakdown.

Q: Does your dad ever talk to you about it?

A: He's not really the sort of man who would. He'll talk about things that aren't really on the subject of divorce like football. He's not like my mum who'll understand; who'll sit down and talk to me and understand what I'm saying. He'll just sit down and talk to me about something I don't want to talk about. So, no, I don't really talk to my dad about things like that.

> Louise, aged 12

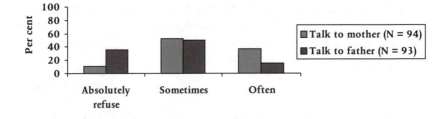

*Figure 2.6 How much do you want to talk to your mother/father about the divorce?*

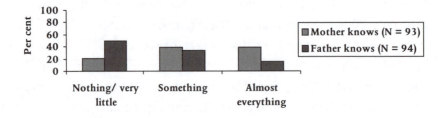

*Figure 2.7 How well does your mother/father know your feelings about the divorce?*

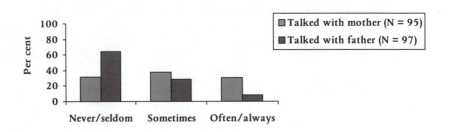

*Figure 2.8 How often have you and your mother/father talked about your feelings about the divorce?*

It was in the minority of cases where children were told about the separation by both parents together.

> They called Sarah and I downstairs. We were playing. Dad was sitting on one chair, Mummy was sitting on the settee, and they said they're getting divorced. I started crying like mad. I just didn't believe it.

Michael, aged 10

A:   They just sat me down. It was in the evening. He said 'You'll find that my stuff is not upstairs anymore' and I started getting all upset and I was like, 'Why?' and he goes, 'Oh because I'm just going to go and live with Nana because me and your mum don't love each other any more'. So I like, burst into tears then and I was really upset.

Q:   Did they tell you together?

A:   Yeah. But mostly Dad did all the talking really. He just said they couldn't live with each other any more and he made it clear that it wasn't our fault. He said, 'It's got nothing to do with you'. And he said, 'It's not as though there's anyone else, or anything like that'. He just said he just couldn't live with my mum any more.

Julie, aged 12

When both parents had chosen to talk to their children, it was more usual for each of them to do so separately.

Q:   Who told you about it?

A:   They both did really. They did it at different times. They said that they don't think they could get on very well and they thought that it'd be better if they split up.

Ellie, aged 10

One consequence of telling children separately was that, due to the parents' different perspectives, children ended up with apparently different accounts of what was happening and why. For example, Rosie's father explained to her his reasons for ending the marriage a few weeks before leaving and without her mother's knowledge. When her mother came to explain, she gave different reasons, leaving Rosie confused and questioning her father's honesty.

> When my mum had gone out, he [Daddy] said that Mummy and Daddy didn't love each other anymore. But my mummy a few weeks ago said that that was a lie. She said that she still loved Daddy and that Daddy had been telling a lie to me. And a few weeks ago he said that he left Mummy 'cos he felt that he wasn't being loved. Mummy said that was a lie as well. So sometimes, when my dad says something I think, I don't know if he's telling the truth.
>
> Rosie, aged 10

We shall see later (Chapter 4) that for Rosie this confusion and doubt would affect how she came to relate to her father and his new partner. For other children, what parents might have regarded as well-intentioned attempts to shield their children could be perceived as further examples of a breach of trust. Despite parents' beliefs to the contrary, 29.1 per cent of children whom we spoke to reported that no one had told them that separation was imminent (see Figure 2.1). Sometimes this was almost inevitable in that one parent left very suddenly. In these circumstances it often fell to the remaining parent to explain.

> Well, she was crying and I said, 'What's the matter?' Richard [brother] was cuddling her. So I said, 'What's happened?' and I said, 'Where's Dad?' and she just started telling me about what he said and I said, 'Is he coming back?' And she said, 'Well, I don't know'. That's when it all happened. He phoned up the next morning and said, 'Oh, I won't be coming back'. We just begged him for the whole, whole day. We started ringing him up every minute of the day, to say, 'Please, please come back' and we were all crying our eyes out.
>
> Cathy, aged 13

A few children described how they had been told about the separation over the telephone.

> Well, I found out that they were splitting up over the telephone. Dad rang us up to say that he wasn't coming back. That's all we heard for a while.
>
> Rachel, aged 10

Some parents apparently tried to break the news more gently by telling their children in a circuitous manner. For example, Sian's mum took her to see her new house as a prelude to telling her about the forthcoming separation.

> One day after school, Mummy just took me round to the bungalow, and she said, 'This is where we are going to live' and I said, 'What, you mean, for a few weeks?' I thought, like, just for a few weeks so that Mummy could have a bit of a rest from Daddy and she said, 'No, forever' and I was a bit surprised.
>
> Sian, aged 8

Similar attempts to insinuate changes into the child's life with the introduction of new partners met with similar responses, as we shall see in Chapter 4. Despite any anticipation by the child or the degree to which parents told children what was happening, the majority of children still found the reality of finding out very hard.

> The worst part about it was the night when my mum and dad really broke up. That's the worst part. Because we were in the front room, me, Jason [brother] and Katie [sister] and we were just really worried and frightened and stuff like that.
>
> Stewart, aged 10

> Well, I knew when I was about nine, I knew something was going to go wrong. I knew that my mum was getting angry and upset about it, so I knew that it was going to end in something like this. But divorce, I didn't think it would quite be divorce. I thought maybe my dad would have some sense to sort out his problems.
>
> Louise, aged 12

> I did think they were going to break up because I didn't think Dad was going to stand for any of it, but it really hit home when she left.
>
> Susan, aged 14

Like many children, Susan had always assumed that her parents would stay together forever and described her disbelief at finding out her parents were going to split up:

> It feels normal that other people are split up but not YOUR mum and dad. I mean, you think your mum and dad are going to be together forever and you can't believe it's happened.

Characteristically, children described feeling shocked when they found out about their parents' separation. This was particularly evident when the separation was unexpected, for example, when a parent left without warning, or when the separation seemed to be triggered by a single, isolated incident like finding out about an affair.

> I was in bed when he actually left. And he just went in the middle of the night. And in the morning, my mum and me and everyone in my family were crying. I thought he was going to come back later, in about a month or two months or even a week, but nothing happened.
>
> Sarah, aged 8

When children talked about what they were initially told about their parents' separation they recalled being given the information in a very matter-of-fact way with little discussion about their feelings or the potential consequences of the breakdown.

> Mum just explained it to me. Me and your dad are getting divorced. We don't love each other any more. Something like that. Just told me what it was.
>
> Damian, aged 13

> My mum told me. She said 'Rhys', she said, 'We're split up now so me and your dad have decided to get divorced'. And they got divorced.
>
> Rhys, aged 11

This was in contrast to the strong initial response of the children themselves. Most children described feeling sad or upset initially. The majority of children said they had cried on finding out.

> Well, a long, long, long, long cry. Then when he'd gone we stood in the hallway, for quite a while just hugging each other and sobbing our hearts out, you know, it was quite hard.
>
> Julie, aged 12

> I was very upset. I tried to hold it, and I couldn't hold it, so I burst out crying.
>
> Joe, aged 8

> I just sat there feeling really sad. My eyes were watering and I started crying, then there was just me sat there, feeling sad.
>
> Josie, aged 13

Another common initial reaction was a feeling of anger. The anger was usually directed towards the parent whom the children felt was responsible for the family's breakdown.

> I was just crying and everything. I was punching stuff and ripping down stuff. I was just getting all my anger out.
>
> Nick, aged 12

We shall see later how Nick's anger was to get him into fights at school and cause further difficulties in his relationship with his father (Chapter 4).

> Angry! Very angry with my mum and dad. I was like, I didn't speak to my mum and dad for a couple of days. But I didn't really, like, take my anger out on them. I just felt it inside; that I was annoyed with them because they got a divorce.
>
> Sioned, aged 12

The emotional shock experienced by children might still be overlooked even when parents had attempted to talk directly to their children about the separation, rather than simply present the separation in a rather 'matter-of-fact' way as some parents did.

> Just very empty and lonely – as though I had no one to talk to. Because you know, all my mum's family were, like, comforting her, and my dad's family was comforting him and I thought that me and Neil [brother] had no one to go to 'cos like there were sides. But there wasn't really – it's just like if we went over to Mum's you know, they were too busy looking after Mum. And I know that Mum felt sorry for us as well but it's like I felt lonely – as though I had no one to go to and talk to 'cos I felt that Mum had to be comforted and Dad had to be comforted and I thought there's no one in between for me and Neil.
>
> Sioned, aged 12

A small number of children reported feeling relief when they first found out. In these cases, the children usually felt that family circumstances had become intolerable and so were glad that things were finally going to change.

> Relieved and upset. I was just really upset at the time. But then it took a lot of pressure off the whole family.
>
> Susan, aged 13

Confusion and uncertainty were also common after the initial shock.

> Very confused, like I didn't expect it and everyone else had their mum
> and dad together. So it was very difficult. I got upset sometimes. Wished
> they were together and it was very difficult to cope.
>
> Gareth, aged 15

A:   I think I was probably confused and, you know, I did wonder about
the future. I was curious about the future you know, what was going
to be happening to us and what was going to be happening with
Dad and things like that.

Q:   Did you have any thoughts about what might happen?

A:   Well, I thought BAD things. I could just imagine Dad being really,
really lonely all by himself all the time but then I realised that
wouldn't be true 'cos he'd find somebody else.

> Will, aged 14

Robin's initial feeling was a sense of injustice of the situation, he felt that it
was simply 'not fair' that this should be happening to him:

Q:   Do you remember how you reacted when you found out that they
were getting a divorce?

A:   I wasn't talking, for about two days. Some tried to talk and I just
went up to my room and shut the door.

Q:   What did you feel when you were up in your room?

A:   Everything's not fair.

> Robin, aged 10

Several other children submerged or compounded their own anxiety with
a concern for their parents. We shall see later how such concern could also
lead to children being very protective of their 'wronged' parent (Chapter
4).

Once the initial shock had begun to subside, children described a
range of feelings as they began to come to terms with finding out about
their parents' separation. Most children described feeling a mixture of a
sense of relief that the arguing, and sometimes the violence, was over and
at the same time, a continuing sense of loss, sadness and uncertainty about
the future.

I was sad but I could understand because they'd been arguing and everything. I was a bit, I was sort of glad that they wouldn't be arguing all the time.

Becky, aged 12

Pretty horrible, upset obviously. I felt a big mixture of emotions in my head. I didn't know whether I was happy that it was over because I didn't have to keep anything bottled up anymore; whether I was sad because I wanted Mum and Dad to be together, and just a whole load of things.

Sean, aged 14

The majority of children referred to such a period of being unsettled, sometimes marked by disturbed sleep patterns. During this time they were trying to come to terms simultaneously with the changes happening in their family; with their new living and contact arrangements; with coping with their ongoing feelings of uncertainty about the future and dealing with the continued confusion and worry surrounding the breakdown.

I was confused. I didn't know what I wanted. I didn't know whether I wanted to live with my dad. I knew I wanted to live with my mum. She's the one that didn't leave me. But I'm not sure. I really hate my dad now for what he did. I've realised that he left and he left for another woman. He didn't stay with his kids. He didn't want us any more. And for a whole year he didn't talk to us one bit.

Cathy, aged 13

Just don't really want my parents to get divorced. Well, in a way I sort of do, 'cos there's things that they did, that I want to sort of like 'stop'. Sometimes they sort of like, have the odd little argument, round here and if they get divorced all those problems will be solved really.

Jonathan, aged 12

During this period of readjustment, many of the children talked of their concerns for their parents' happiness and how they worried about them being lonely in the future.

I felt sad for my mum 'cos I thought, 'Oh, she'll be really upset about it'. As long as my mum was all right that was the main thing.

Viv, aged 14

I think it's what I've come to now. But I've always thought, whenever Mum was happy, I was happy. But it took me like a couple of weeks to sort of like say, well, as long as Mum is happy then it doesn't matter what has happened. But at the same time, as long as Dad's happy. But I can't have both, so as long as Mum is happy.

Sophie, aged 15

Many of the children were also trying to deal with strong feelings of loss. They missed their absent parent.

Just missing my dad really. Not wanting him to go. I mean it's all very well me seeing him twice a week, but that's really not enough. I mean, you'd like him there everyday, you know. And he says he misses himself, the birthdays, and everything. OK, he can come down and spend a certain amount of time with us and all, but he can't be there in the morning, on Christmas morning, to see us waking up and everything. So basically just missing him really.

Julie, aged 12

There was a small group of children for whom readjustment proved particularly difficult, for whom the feelings of upset, anger and confusion lasted longer.

A:   I always used to get these tempers and I used to have tantrums and everything. I used to like rip out my radiator and everything. I was mad at him. I felt all depressed and everything. Like if anything went wrong, like I'd start crying and throwing the tantrums really.

Q:   Do you ever feel like that now?

A:   Yeah. Sometimes like. I like feel very angry and I shout and everything. But it's not as bad.

Q:   What's helped you kind of calm down?

A:   'cos now I started to realise things, I've grown older. I've found out more stuff about what happened.

Noel, aged 12

A few children continued to feel isolated and could see only the negative side of what had happened for a considerable period.

Like I was the only person that's parents had got divorced and I just felt really sad and lonely thinking, 'Oh, this is gonna be horrible' – you know. Mum's on her own, Dad's on his own and I wanted them to get back together again. And all my friends at school's parents have got, you know, they're all together and really happy – one nice happy family and it just wasn't working for mine.

Sioned, aged 12

A few children also found it very hard to accept that their parents really had separated and experienced continued 'magical' hopes of reconciliation. These children recalled feeling that the whole experience was a dream from which they would wake, and then it would all be over.

*A:* I first thought that I would wake up tomorrow morning and everything would be OK. I keeped (sic) on thinking the same thing, and I still do.

*Q:* Do you still think that that might happen?

*A:* I'd like it to happen that I'd wake up and think, 'Oh,' and I'd just woken up, it was all a dream, a nightmare.

Dan, aged 10

Many of the children highlighted the importance both of being told what was happening, and of being given an explanation of why the changes were necessary.

*Q:* Do you think you really understood?

*A:* Yeah, probably because I mean, he [Dad] explained it quite well. He made sure I understood quite well.

*Q:* Do you think that helped, the fact that they actually sat you down, and explained it all to you before he went?

*A:* Yeah, because he could've easily just taken off, without any warning. But yeah, I would've rather that he done it like that 'cos then we got to say goodbye properly and everything.

Julie, aged 12

At the height of the emotional crisis of divorce, and afterwards for most children, as well as identifying the need for emotional support, children wanted to be told what was happening. In order to restore some kind of balance, a degree of cognitive control over events was needed. Being left out of the explanations could feel very like being left out altogether.

> It was like, 'Oh well, it's not really your problem; you're just not going to be affected by it. You don't have to go through all the divorce things'. But, no one seemed to realise I was sort of there. They were all concerned with what they were doing.

> Libby, aged 13

In contrast to the children's need, as we have suggested, it was apparent that many of the parents were choosing not to give detailed information in an attempt to protect their children from additional worry or upset. Some parents failed to appreciate that they were compounding their children's confusion and their uncertainty about the future.

*A:* I thought it was all fine, except for the fact that they were all SHOUTING at each other down the phone and stuff like that and knowing that Ray [father] wouldn't let me know things; hide it all from me. I could see what was going on but he just wouldn't tell me.

*Q:* What sort of things did you want to know?

*A:* Enough to keep me not confused. You know, it would be all this rowing and stuff and it would be like, 'What?! What's this about now?' And he wouldn't explain anything to me; you know, when is this going to be ended, and stuff like that.

> Oliver, aged 13

Having what they considered to be a reasonable explanation for why their parents had decided to separate appeared to help children come to terms with what was happening.

> I suppose I wouldn't of minded sort of knowing 'why' at the time 'cos my mum just said, 'Oh, we're separating'. So I suppose I'd really liked to have known why, sort of then. Instead, I sort of figured it out.

> Helen, aged 15

The children stressed the importance of being told about the changes *before* they happened. One extreme version of this was when a parent left home without telling their children. What was particularly difficult for some children was that they had not been given the opportunity to 'say goodbye'.

Cathy felt very strongly that she needed her father to give her an explanation, that she needed him to reassure her that he still cared, and that she needed him to apologise for what he had done.

Q: Did you ever talk to your dad about it?

A: Yeah. I've said, 'Why did you leave me? Who did you love more?' And everything.

Q: Did he ever give you any answers to these questions?

A: No. He's never ever said 'Sorry' or 'I love you' or anything. He's never ever said anything. He's never asked us anything.

Q: What would you like to hear him say?

A: 'I'm sorry for leaving you' and, 'I didn't mean it'. I mean I still hate him! But he's never ever, ever said sorry to me. Or said, 'I love you'. I said, 'Who do you love more? Me or Tina?' [new partner] and he said, 'I can't answer that question'. I'd just like to know that he still loves me and he still likes me.

Q: Did he ever give you a satisfactory answer to your question?

A: No. I said, 'Why have you left me?' And he's said, ''cos I found another person' or something. That was all he wanted to say. He never wanted to talk to me. I think it was his negative points. He just didn't want us to say anything.

Q: Do you think it would've helped more if he'd explained why?

A: I mean, I knew why, but I wanted to hear it from him. I didn't just want to hear it from my mum who lives here.

Cathy, aged 13

While most children expressed the need to be kept informed throughout the process of family breakdown, a number also described difficulties they had experienced when their parents had tried to talk to them. One of the issues children highlighted was the difficulty parents sometimes had in giving age-appropriate information. Anne, who had a much younger brother and sister reported how difficult it had been for her mum to explain. Her mum had sat all three children down together but then found it difficult to find a way to explain so that they would all understand.

> Well, she's sat me down with Jake [brother] and Amy [sister] as well but she can't really explain things because they're too little to understand.
>
> Anne, aged 11

While the majority of children agreed that a regular supply of information would have helped them deal with the changes in their family, Rhiannon felt that being given too much information at any one time could be detrimental. For her, picking up information about her family's breakdown in a more piecemeal fashion was easier. She preferred not to be given too much information at once as this allowed her to come to terms with things more gradually.

> A:   I think it was probably listening to other people talking and then realising, and little things like that. They all sort of link together, then I realised what it meant. I think it just sort of gradually 'builded' (sic) up. Built up and got used to it.
>
> Q:   Would you have liked someone to have sat you down and explained?
>
> A:   No, in some ways it was easier that way. I learnt gradually what was going on. I don't think I would've liked to have been sat down and told what was going on.
>
> Rhiannon, aged 14

Some of the children had appreciated their parents' efforts to protect them from additional upset by not telling them too much.

> I think it was all right because what I didn't know didn't hurt me really. If I'd known more about it, I would've been more upset about it.
>
> Libby, aged 13

Many of the children we spoke to said they would have liked to ask their parents questions but found it hard to do so. A few children, completely unprepared for their parents' separation, were simply too shocked to ask questions when they first found out.

Q: Did you ask them lots of questions that time?

A: No, I was just speechless. It was all a bit too much of a shock at the time.

Michael, aged 10

Others were worried they would upset themselves or their parents by asking questions.

Q: Have you talked to your mum about it?

A: No, not particularly.

Q: Why is that?

A: 'cos I knew that I'd get upset and I knew that Mum would get upset as well.

Sean, aged 14

Some children simply did not seem to know how to ask their parents questions when they wanted to know something about the breakdown. Some did not want to ask because they feared the consequences of doing so; others felt it best just to 'keep quiet'.

Q: Have you ever asked your dad why?

A: No, 'cos I'm afraid that he might not see us ever again.

Q: Why do you think that?

A: Because I might upset his feelings and he might not start to like me any more and things like that.

James, aged 9

Whilst children's accounts of their parents' separation might remain incomplete for a variety of reasons, some derived from their parents' inability or reluctance to keep them informed, others derived from reticence or reluctance on the child's part to ask questions or engage in 'difficult' conversations with their parents. Children nonetheless still formed opinions about why their parents' marriage was ending. Many children described a gradual breakdown in their parents' relationship; others attributed the separation to the specific behaviours of the parent whom they blamed for the breakdown; and others were unsure why their parents had decided to separate.

Many children believed their parents' arguments to be the root cause of the separation – the cause rather than the symptom of the other underlying problems with the relationship.

> My mum said, if they lived here together, that they'd be arguing all the time and I'd rather they lived apart, than stay together and argue all the time. It'd just be horrible.
>
> Ted, aged 10

Other children described a more gradual breakdown of their parents' relationship. Some felt that their parents simply did not 'get on' anymore and others had gradually witnessed them growing apart or felt that they were just 'not suited'.

> I think they don't get on as well as other parents do really. They don't really suit. They don't really have the same things in common. When I was quite young I thought that they were OK together but then as I got older I could see that they weren't right together.
>
> Ellie, aged 10

> Ben's parents were splitting up and I asked, 'Do you know why?' And he goes, ''cos like my mum's into hippy stuff and my dad's into cars, they're just not suited'. Then I spoke to Mum about that, and she said, 'It's like your dad, we didn't have common interests and things'. 'Cos my dad was a late worker and Mum was a day worker and they never spent time together and it just lost the romance. They just didn't get on.
>
> Damian, aged 13

A small number of children felt that their parents had separated because they did not love each other any more.

> They separated because my dad said he'd just stopped loving my mum 'cos they been together now much longer than he'd really wanted to. He said he stayed, just because of the children. You know, us two. He said he didn't really want to leave when we were too young, he explained to me that he was thinking of leaving quite a long time ago.
>
> Sally, aged 12

Some children attributed the separation to particular behaviours or incidents for which they usually blamed one specific parent. Specific behaviours and incidents children cited as factors in their parents' separation included: the use and abuse of alcohol, domestic violence, financial difficulties and infidelity. Some children blamed themselves. Six months before her parents' separation, Cathy dreamt that her parents would divorce, as a consequence she felt she had caused it to happen. She subsequently needed professional counselling to help her deal with these feelings.

> Well, I had a dream about it, so I blamed myself for about half a year. It was about a month before it all happened, I dreamt that my mum and dad were getting divorced. I just felt it was my fault 'cos I had the dream. No one else did.
>
> Cathy, aged 13

Consistently, however, children expressed the view that they wanted to know what was happening. Not only would this have helped them deal with their shock, sadness and anxiety for the future, it might also have helped shape the pattern of future relationships.

> Most of it went over my head, but actually being able to see what was going on was quite nice because then I didn't feel like away from the problem. I was, well, not part of it but I was more in than I was out.
>
> Sophie, aged 15

> *A:* I just wanted to know why she did it. I wanted some answers and Mum didn't want to give me any answers. It would've been better if she'd told me then maybe we'd have a closer relationship now.
>
> *Q:* Do you think if she'd sat down and explained it to you that it would've helped?
>
> *A:* Yeah, I think it would've 'cos if we knew the truth, then we could've just cleared the air but that didn't happen, it's still going on now. You never talk about it, but it's still there.
>
> Susan, aged 14

In the absence of information and explanation, children gleaned what they could from a variety of sources. Many had drawn on their friends' first-hand experiences of family breakdown.

> Because if you do get divorced, you might not even get to see your mum or dad again, like my friend; 'cos her mum and dad got divorced and she didn't get to see her dad again.
>
> Maggie, aged 10

It was clear also that a number of children had learnt about separation and divorce at school. Some had used their teachers as a source of information; others had learnt about family breakdown through school lessons.

Q: What would YOU say if you had to explain it to me?

A: When one parent leaves the other and they don't see each other very often.

Q: Where did you learn that from?

A: I was kind of told it.

Q: Who told you?

A: My teacher.

Q: Did you learn about it at school?

A: Yeah. We watched a video and then we talked about it.

> Dean, aged 9

A few children had read books about separation and divorce; their parents had either given the books to them or they had got them themselves from the library.

> My mother brought a book from the library. It said all about divorce. It was just stuff which tells you all about divorce.
>
> Aaron, aged 12

One of the most common sources of information was television. Some children had picked up information from soap operas or television chat shows, which they then used to help them understand family breakdown and what was happening in their own family.

Q: Did she explain what divorce means?

A: Yeah. Well, when they split up for good. I already knew. I used to watch these films, like Jerry Springer and all that. When they were divorcing and stuff.

Ricky, aged 12

A few had watched films based on the subject of family breakdown. It was interesting to note that Abby preferred to believe the information she gained from watching a film rather than what her dad told her:

No. I knew they were going to court and stuff like that 'cos I seen it in a film *Mrs Doubtfire* about that. But, I asked my dad about that, and he said, 'No! We don't go to court at all'. I said, 'I know you do 'cos I'd seen it on the telly'.

Abby, aged 11

## Discussion

Parental divorce constitutes a moment of emotional shock and high anxiety for most children. This is likely to be the case irrespective of whether the final sequence of events is anticipated or not. Certainly, most children had become aware that something was seriously wrong in their parents' relationship before separation occurred. Children knew that something was happening. The children we spoke to seemed broadly to agree that important in reducing the sense of crisis was a much greater flow of information and explanation than some children actually received. This may be as important as reassurance and support at a more obviously emotional level. One can imagine how difficult this must be in a climate where a whole range of emotional needs are struggling to be met and one should recognise that not all children are able or want to engage in 'difficult' discussion with their parents. It is important to recognise that while we do detect clear patterns in the responses that children made to us and we do find commonalities in their experiences, children are no more an homogeneous category than any other and individual responses cannot easily be predicted. Parents and other adults will still need to differentiate their responses to children and to take into account their uniqueness. Therefore, almost any dialogue would seem preferable to the uncertainty that derives from being excluded from the process. Obtaining some cognitive control of the crisis (an important component of returning to a 'steady state'), especially in the absence of any immediate resolution of the emotional upset, anger, feelings of injustice and feelings of loss, is important to children. They express a need to be kept informed and involved. As we shall see, meeting this need has implications for the nature and quality of children's subsequent relationships with their parents.

An awareness of how far children had recovered a 'balance' in their lives should also influence the pace and timing of any formal intervention during the critical phase in which children begin to absorb the fact that their parents are separating or divorcing. We do not pretend that under-standing and respecting children's own emotional 'pace' is easy. The children's accounts presented here are a reminder that we have to recognise the difficulty that children have in expressing their emotions and are an incentive to be sensitive to their use of metaphor and alternative forms of expressing emotion, like crying, for example. In this chapter we have also begun to reflect the fact that children are able to demonstrate a sympathy for and understanding of their parents, even in the midst of their own upset.

From the moment that children become aware of their parents' separation they become 'involved', at least emotionally, in the process of their parents' divorce. This can be a confused, isolated and exceptionally sad experience, especially if children are not told what is going on around them. We will look later (Chapter 6) at how children seek support and come to terms with the events unfolding around them. For most children, however, the next stage involves telling others what is happening in their lives. This is the subject of the next chapter.

# Chapter 3

# *Telling Others*

We have seen how 'being told' is important to children in managing the immediate consequences of their parents' separation. It is an important part of regaining cognitive control of a potentially psychologically threatening experience. Despite the fact that many children are left with an inadequate sense of what is happening around them, one of the more immediate tasks facing them once the crisis of their parents' divorce has arisen, is deciding what and how to 'tell others'. This is something children are faced with almost immediately, no matter what they have themselves been told. In this chapter, we will examine whom children tell, why and in what circumstances.

Perhaps it is not surprising that many children just had to tell someone what was happening to them.

Q: Did you tell anyone?

A: Yeah, one of my friends.

Q: Just one of them?

A: Yeah.

Q: Why that friend in particular?

A: I don't know. I just wanted to get it out.

Andy, aged 14

In the immediate aftermath of their parents' separation, this pattern of children telling one or possibly a few close friends was the most common amongst both boys and girls of all ages.

Q: Once your mum and dad had split up, did you tell anybody what had happened?

A: I just told my closest friends.

Q: Why was that?

A: I think I was like, I didn't want everybody to find out. I just wanted a few people to know.

Nick, aged 12

Q: Did you tell anyone that Mum and Mike were getting divorced?

A: My school best friend. I kept it a secret from a lot of school friends.

Stewart, aged 9

It is important to note that the majority of children (67%) (see Figure 3.1) turned to their friends as their primary confidant. We will note at several points in succeeding chapters the key role played by children's friends in managing the experience of parental separation. Most children were careful to tell only their 'best friend', those whom they could trust. It was clearly important to children in the immediate aftermath of the crisis that only a few people, outside the family, should know. For example, only three children (see Figure 3.1) were prepared to tell 'anyone' (including class mates) about what had happened.

Q: Were there some people you kept it a secret from?

A: Yeah, people who are like blabbermouths, who just go round and like, twist it around; just lies and that and just tell everyone.

Catherine, aged 12

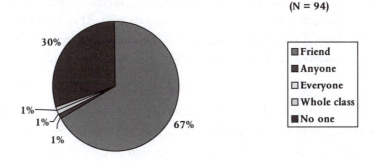

*Figure 3.1 Who did you tell about the divorce?*

Most children were careful where they placed their trust.

Q: You mentioned Luke as a 'best friend'. Did you tell him?

A: Not at the time 'cos I didn't properly know him then. But when we started to become friends, I really trusted him and I started telling him things.

Q: What sort of things might you tell him?

A: Like Mum and Dad split up and getting a divorce. Some secrets that I knew he could keep.

Rory, aged 12

A: I told my best friend and that was about it really, 'cos I could trust her and I didn't want her to say anything.

Ellie, aged 10

Restricting the flow of information may have helped children 'contain' the crisis in which they found themselves, allowing them to exercise some actual as well as cognitive control over what was happening.

Over 84 per cent of children reported that friends understood their feelings although some took the view that people who had not been through it could not really understand what it was like or how it 'felt'.

Q: Did you think they [friends] understood about it?

A: No, I don't think they could fully because they haven't had it happen, but to a certain extent they understood. But they couldn't understand the sort of emotional side of it. They could understand like all parents splitting up; that's about it but they didn't understand what sort of goes through people's heads.

Sean, aged 14

Reflecting this, children were generally more willing to talk about what was happening with children who had themselves experienced family breakdown as 'they knew what it was like'. Many children also believed that those who had 'been there' would better understand the need to respect privacy.

Q: Did you tell anyone that your mum and dad were going to get divorced?

A: Yeah, I told Phil. His parents are divorced so he knew what it was going to be like and that; and I told Pete 'cos I know him, and he promised not to say anything.

Q: Did you ask him not to say anything?

A: Yeah. I just wanted people not to know. 'Cos they would all ask me questions.

George, aged 10

A: I felt OK 'cos I only told the people whose mum and dad weren't together first 'cos they told me, and I didn't go blabbing off to everybody. So I told them, knowing that they wouldn't go blabbing off. They'd know the feeling that you wouldn't want other people to know, and things like that.

Catherine, aged 12

The main benefit of talking to others who had 'been there' was that it provided children with a context within which to place their own experience. Thus their unique circumstances, feelings and emotions could appear less extraordinary. This helped a number of children recover the sense of 'normality' most so actively sought.

Q: Did you tell anyone that your mum and dad were splitting up?

A: Yeah. Loads of my friends at school have had the same things happening. Sort of two or three times. I would just talk to them about it and everything and they were cool with it and everything.

Q: Do you think they understood?

A: Yeah, 'cos they had all been through it and they were like exactly the same as I was.

Stewart, aged 9

Amongst the children who spoke to us, 30 per cent (see Figure 3.1) reported that they had told no one about their parents' separation. Most of these children wanted to keep the information about what had happened a secret from everyone.

Q: Did you tell anyone that your mum and dad had split up?

A: No!

Q: You kept it a secret from everyone?

A: Yes.

Ralph, aged 8

Q: Have you told anybody about your mum and Andy divorcing?

A: No, I don't want to tell anybody.

Ollie, aged 9

Often this would be because the child regarded the matter as essentially a 'family affair' and, as such, a private matter. Ralph, aged 8, continued:

Q: Did you tell anyone that your mum and dad were getting divorced?

A: No.

Q: Did you want to keep it a secret from other people?

A: Yeah.

Q: Why did you want to keep it a secret?

A: So it was at home; I don't like telling them about things like that.

In Michael's (aged 10) comments, there is the familiar echo of the desire to 'contain' the flow of information about his parents' separation:

Q: Did you tell anyone that your mum and dad were splitting up?

A: No! Just wanted to keep it to our family. I wanted to keep it to myself, not telling everyone with them spreading it.

Q: Is there anybody that you've told outside the family?

A: No! No one.

Sometimes children's reasons for not telling others reflected their personal difficulty in talking about what had happened and also their anxiety over the possible consequences of telling others. One common reason the children gave was their fear of becoming upset if they talked about their parents' separation or divorce to others.

Q: Did you tell friends or anybody like that?

A: My mum actually told my friends that my parents are divorced, 'cos, like, they were actually wondering where my dad was and I couldn't actually tell them 'cos I wasn't up to it. I was like upset and couldn't talk about it.

Gareth, aged 15

Q: How do you feel when you have to tell people about it?

A: Quite upset because when I just talk about it, I just remember the day and start crying.

Ann, aged 8

A small number of children described being embarrassed or ashamed about what was happening in their family.

I told everything to all my best friends but the rest of them I didn't really say 'cos all their parents were together and it's like shameful.

Samantha, aged 13

For some children the fact that they themselves knew very little about what was happening added to their difficulties when it came to talking to other people.

Q: Why did you wait before you told people?

A: Just confused and didn't have a clue what was going on so I couldn't tell anyone about it then.

Anne, aged 11

Even amongst those children who had confided in their best friend, in a small circle of friends or in a trusted adult, there was an awareness of the possible negative consequences of telling others. The difficulties of finding an appropriate balance between retaining their privacy, keeping control of information and getting a degree of emotional support will be discussed further in Chapter 6.

For a large number of children, the fear of being teased or rejected by their friends or their peers at school created real difficulties in being able to talk freely about what had happened.

Well, I've kept it a secret from my worst friend 'cos he'll probably tease me and all that. I told one of my friends and he called me, 'Dad-less'.

Johnny, aged 10

Q: What did you think would happen if you told other people?

A: Maybe, make fun of me 'cos my dad didn't live with me anymore. Something like that.

David, aged 11

Q: Was there anybody that you didn't tell?

A: I didn't tell everybody, I only told my best friends 'cos the other children made fun of me and goes, *(singing)* 'Oh, Jennifer hasn't got a dad any more', because some of my friends would do that.

Jennifer, aged 9

Another common fear children expressed was that they might be thought of as 'different' or 'weird'. This was an important consideration for most children, especially teenagers.

Q: Why do you think you didn't tell people?

A: Being different; 'cos everyone else's mum and dad were together.

Sophie, aged 15

Q: What did you think would happen if you told people?

A: Don't know; just that they'd say 'you're weird' or something like that.

Samantha, aged 13

A few of the children said that their fear of upsetting parents or being 'told off' by them prevented them telling others.

Q: Why don't you want to tell anyone?

A: 'Cos I feel as if they're going to tell somebody and then I could get into a lot of trouble with my mother.

Ollie, aged 9

Q: Have your mum or dad asked you if you've told other people about them splitting up?

A: My ma has and I've told her and she says 'it's all right'. But if my dad asked me I wouldn't tell him 'cos he'd like smack me or something for telling other people.

Charlie, aged 11

Other children were inhibited by the concern they felt for their parents' happiness. The following is just one example of the care children took for the emotional welfare of their parents, others of which we report later.

Q: Did you tell anyone that your mum and dad were splitting up?

A: No 'cos my mum wouldn't be happy.

Stewart, aged 9

Yet another reason some children gave for not telling others was that they felt no real need to do so.

A: I only told about five people.

Q: Why was that?

A: Oh, I didn't feel the need to.

Damian, aged 13

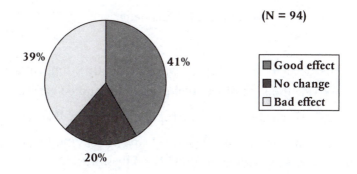

*Figure 3.2 Effect of divorce on relationship with friends*

Thirty nine per cent of children reported that their parents' divorce had had a negative effect on their relationships with their friends (see Figure 3.2). However, almost all of the children (94%) reported that they liked talking to their friends as much after their parents' separation as before and 96 per cent reported that they liked playing with their friends as much as they did previously.

We have already reported that the most frequently presented reason the children gave for wanting to tell someone about their parents' separation was their own need 'to get it out'.

Q: Did you tell your friends instantly?

A: Yeah. I really just wanted to get it out. That's right, I think the first day I went back into school after it happened.

Sally, aged 12

It kinda meant I had someone to share it with, so you know, I just wasn't keeping it inside me.

Robert, aged 13

To some children the benefit of 'getting it out' was obvious, even beforehand.

Q: How did you feel when you had to tell them?

A: I didn't have to I just wanted to.

Q: Why did you want to?

A: 'Cos it would make me feel better.

Henry, aged 8

The need to vent feelings was sufficiently strong in some children to override the kind of parental prohibitions noted earlier.

Q: When your parents first split up, did you tell anyone?

A: My mother said, 'Don't tell anyone yet'. But I had to tell someone; I was just crying, so I told Jason [best friend].

Claire, aged 10

As well as being trusted not to ridicule, reject or breach their confidence, the impartiality or neutrality of the confidant was particularly important to children.

Q: Why did you particularly tell Dean? [friend]

A: Well, I needed to talk to someone about it and there was no point in talking about it to my mother so, I confided in Dean.

Q: Did it help?

A: Yeah, 'cos I got it out of my system and he told me not to worry about it, and if I ever wanted to speak, to talk to him.

Daniel, aged 14

Choosing whom to tell allowed children to vent their feelings safely whilst still allowing them to retain some control of the consequences. Additionally, for some children, telling others was a means of securing support, even advice, when they were upset, worried or confused.

Q: Did you keep it a secret from anyone that your mum and dad were getting divorced?

A: Not really 'cos I really wanted to tell my next-door neighbour because if they would know, they would know to give me some advice. I wanted to tell my friends as well so they might give me advice too.

Lucy, aged 8

Nick, who as we have seen was struggling with some very powerful negative feelings towards his father, also found his friends supportive:

Q: Did you tell anybody what had happened?

A: Yeah, 'cos like at that time I was in [local] school and I had best friends. So I told them and they were like really supportive, 'cos a lot of their parents were divorced already. They knew what I was going through and stuff.

Nick, aged 12

Other reasons children gave for telling were more pragmatic.

Q: How did you feel about telling people?

A: I don't know. It's something that's true so they'll find out anyway so I might as well tell them.

Will, aged 14

It is important to note that children usually had very clear expectations of what they wanted to achieve by talking to others. They knew when and from whom they wanted advice or practical assistance. They also knew from whom and when they just wanted someone to listen, respecting their confidence, maintaining their privacy, and so helping them to recover their 'balance'. Children's capacity to discriminate in their help-seeking behaviour has been reported elsewhere (see Butler and Williamson 1994, for example) and, as we shall see below, adults in particular were not always sufficiently sensitive to or respectful of children's own assessments of what they needed and how they wanted to be treated to be in a position to offer the help children wanted.

The timing of telling others was important for many children. For example, some of the children talked of their need to come to terms with what was happening before they felt able to tell others. The period children said they had needed (or would need) before being comfortable talking to others varied from a few days to several years.

Q: Why was it that you didn't want other people to know?

A: I just don't think I was ready to tell everyone about it.

Ellie, aged 10

Q: Did you find that you decided not to tell people?

A: No, it was just I wanted to get to terms with it first.

Josie, aged 13

Our general view, as indicated in Chapter 2, is that most of the children we spoke to seemed to experience difficulties in knowing *how* to talk about what had happened, even when they had clearly decided to talk. Very few of the children had ever had the experience of talking about such a sensitive and, for some, such an upsetting subject as their own family's breakdown. Not unreasonably, a number of them were concerned about the reactions they might provoke.

> I felt inside a bit upset but I said to myself I've got to keep myself together, I just can't you know, get upset about it because they're just going to think, 'Oh my God she's a wimp'; and 'It's a divorce, it's going to happen' so I just felt myself inside feel a bit upset.

Louise, aged 12

A sense of 'awkwardness' often accompanied telling others. This seemed particularly true for boys:

> It was a bit awkward at first. It was like, I don't know, like telling someone, it's just awkward, having to sit there and talk about that but after a while it was fine.

Oliver, aged 13

> Uncomfortable; sort of a matter I wouldn't touch on normally.

Steven, aged 9

> It was a bit strange really, 'cos I didn't know how to, what to say really. It's not something you talk about everyday. It's a bit hard to know what to say.

Ted, aged 12

As a number of children feared, one of the difficulties when telling others was having to deal with questions about what had happened. Many of the children found this annoying and upsetting, particularly when they themselves did not have the answers:

Q: How did you feel when you had to tell people about it?

A: A bit upset by people keep asking questions and I don't know the answers properly.

Luke, aged 11

Q: How do you feel about not telling people?

A: It was OK 'cos I don't get anyone like saying 'why, what, where, when' – like that and I'd be fed up answering them all.

Michael, aged 10

In some circumstances, how children went about telling others was influenced by their parents' views. Claire, aged 10, described some of the difficulties she experienced because her mum asked her to keep what was happening at home a secret from her friends:

Q: Was it difficult not being able to tell people?

A: Yeah, it was because I was so upset that people would ask me what was wrong and I'd say, 'Oh nothing, just one of my pets had gone' or something like that. Having to make up excuses. And when they come up, they say, 'I thought one of your pets had gone'. 'Oh no, we found it in the end.' We had to keep telling them things like that. So it was really difficult to keep secrets.

By comparison, Rhys, also aged 10, described how having a clear explanation from his mother meant that he did not mind telling people:

My mum had explained 'just because we don't love each other anymore it doesn't mean that we don't love you and that you'll be able to see Dad every couple of weeks from now on'. And she said that 'we're better when we're apart' and then I didn't really mind about people knowing.

We have mentioned at several points already how children tried to 'normalise' their experience, to put it into context and actively manage the consequences for them of their parents' separation or divorce. Attempts to normalise are particularly evident in the way children described their reactions to the responses they provoked by 'telling others'. It is important to stress that children were generally appreciative of the efforts that others

– friends, family members and other adults – made to 'look after' them once they had been told what was happening.

> At first because like, I'm a very private person anyway, very sensitive, people were a bit like, treating me like a piece of china. They were very careful around me.
>
> Sophie, aged 15

> I think they treated me more nice. Sort of, kind. Saying 'We know what you're going through, Ellie, so don't worry'.
>
> Ellie, aged 10

> Well, my best friend, when I was a bit upset about it, she comforted me and my second best friend does as well.
>
> Sian, aged 8

However, such 'supportive' responses were not always welcome, particularly when children felt the response was out of keeping with what was 'normal'.

Q: Has anyone treated you differently since they found out?

A: Yeah, not in a horrible way, I think they might have felt sorry for me perhaps but I don't want them to; 'cos it shouldn't make them treat me any differently.

Will, aged 14

A: Some of my aunts, just made a big fuss of me. Which is not really that nice.

Q: What sort of things did they do?

A: Just fuss, like you'd make fuss of a baby. It's hard because you don't want them to and you get fed up with it.

Rachel, aged 10

Children appreciated being treated 'normally'.

Q: When people did find out did they treat you any differently?

A: No, they just treated me normal.

Q: How did you feel about that?

*A:* Well, I was glad they treated me normal, 'cos I didn't really like being treated different.

Josie, aged 13

*A:* I never had a problem with bullying or anything like that. They just treated me the same.

*Q:* Was that a good thing?

*A:* Yeah. I didn't like to be treated special because people don't like to show their true feelings about me or something. They act extra nice. If I say something I shouldn't have said they won't say anything about it; and stuff like that. I just prefer to act normally.

Damian, aged 13

*A:* I said, 'Please don't treat me any different. I'm not any different'. I'm not different to any others. I'm not different to what I was. I haven't changed.

Claire, aged 10

While most of the children we spoke to stressed the need to be treated 'normally', a few greatly appreciated the special attention they received at this time. This was particularly so when children felt they were not receiving sufficient support or attention from their family. Libby, aged 13, talking about the extra attention she received from her schoolmates, said:

> I didn't really mind. It was probably 'cos I wasn't getting any attention at home, I was getting more attention at school from all my friends. People that weren't really even my friends like all the boys were like, 'Oh, I'm so sorry' and stuff.

Unfortunately, some of the children's fears about possible negative consequences of telling people about the family breakdown were realised. A few children experienced situations in which others used the information against them. For example, some of the children were teased at school.

*Q:* Did your friends treat you differently or was it just adults who treated you differently?

*A:*   My friends at one point did. But not nicely. Worse. Well, they're not really my friends – they're just people at school. Used to say, 'Ha ha, I live with my mum and my dad and you only live with your mum'.

Laura, aged 10

Well, my mum told me not to tell many children because, you know, it was private. But I told my best friends and they helped. Though at one time my best friend, and I don't know why she was my best friend now, because she spread it around the school. And everybody knew and some people were making fun of me saying, 'Oh, your parents are divorced, my parents aren't, they're fine'. And that made me even more upset and even more angry with them.

Sioned, aged 12

Although some parents sought to influence their children, the active part played by parents in telling others is perhaps less significant than might have been anticipated. Most parents seem to have left it to the children to decide whom to tell about the separation or divorce. The children thought that most parents just assumed that they would tell people as and when they were ready.

*Q:*   Did your mum or your dad ask if you'd told other people?

*A:*   No, I think they just assumed that we'd tell our friends or whatever. And they knew, some of our friends' parents were split up anyway. So, I think they thought they'd be all right if we sort of chat to our friends about it.

*Q:*   Did they suggest that you tell other people?

*A:*   No, not really. I don't really think I talked to them much when it happened and I can't remember them suggesting to do things or tell people or anything. I think they just let us say what we wanted.

Helen, aged 15

Whilst most parents did not dictate to children about whom they should or should not tell, some gave advice about telling others. A number seemed to be trying to protect their children from the possible negative consequences.

Well, she [mother] said, 'Be careful who you tell'. And, 'If you don't want to tell anyone, don't'.

Louise, aged 12

They just said if you want to tell some people you can. They just said just tell your friends but don't bother, like, telling everyone in the world.

Nichola, aged 14

In a few cases, parents did the telling themselves to save their children from having to do so while others had 'given permission' for their children to tell others what had happened.

No, they just said, 'If you want to talk to people, do'. But, I didn't, really.

Ruth, aged 10

Some actually suggested to their children that it would be a good idea if they told others about what had happened.

Well, they said, 'If you want to tell people and let it out, well, do it then'. So I thought it would make me feel better if I told people.

Tony, aged 10

She says, 'Why don't you try telling your friends?' and, 'What do you think about that idea?' I didn't like it very much but I still did it.

Ryan, aged 8

As noted earlier, a few parents specifically asked their children not to tell people what had happened.

Well, my mum told me not to tell many children because, you know, it was private.

Sioned, aged 12

This is how Rory's mum managed to 'persuade' him not to tell others!

A:    Well, I didn't exactly get blackmailed but my mum said she'd give me a little bit of pocket money – a little bit extra. And I used to always get 50p.

Q: What – if you didn't tell?

A: Yeah.

Rory, aged 12

Some of the parents did, however, go on to acknowledge the potential benefit to their children from telling people outside the family.

I think she was happy that I'd talked to people about it. 'Cos I didn't talk to them about it very much.

Lucy, aged 13

Where parents did become more actively involved was in informing their children's school about the changes occurring in the family. It was clear that in the majority of families, parents made a point of informing the school about what had happened. Only 14 per cent of parents reported that the children's school was not informed. Most parents seemed to do this immediately after the separation.

Q: Did your teachers know?

A: I didn't tell them, because I'd feel a bit strange but Mum did ring up the school, because they said if anything happens like that they'd want to know 'cos it could change your behaviour in lessons or something like that, you know.

Sally, aged 12

However, when parents had informed the school they did not always tell their children that they had done so. A number of the children found out from their teachers rather than their parents that the school had been informed. Nonetheless, the majority of children felt it was important that the school knew what had happened so that their circumstances could be taken into account should the child display any changes in behaviour or performance.

A: Well, my mother, I think told one or two of the teachers; saying like, if his work goes down a little bit, not to worry too much, 'cos it's the divorce.

Q: Did that help?

*A:* It helped a bit. Yeah, 'cos I knew, like, if I'd done something wrong and I was in a mood, because of the divorce, they would understand.

Daniel, aged 14

*Q:* Do you think schools, teachers should be told when this is happening?

*A:* Er, yeah, 'cos they could help you. Like lay off a bit. Like instead of giving you detentions or staying behind at break and stuff like that they could say, 'Right, what's the problem?' and you say, 'Well, I've had a bad night with my mum and dad'. 'Right, come and see me at break to talk about it.'

Sam, aged 11

Although most children felt the school should know, their opinions differed as to whether teachers should then become involved. Some clearly felt that they could talk to their teachers and that teachers were a useful source of support.

*A:* Mum came in one day and told my main teacher. Then I did talk to another teacher about it, as well.

*Q:* Did the teacher your mum told say anything to you about it?

*A:* Yeah, she did talk to me, like, ask me how I was and everything. So that was quite helpful. We had, like, a step-in teacher and I talked to her quite a lot 'cos she was really nice. She just sort of listened.

Elizabeth, aged 13

*A:* Yeah, because I liked my teacher. He was really nice; it was good to know that he understood and was talking to me about it. It was quite nice to know that I wasn't on my own.

*Q:* Better in a way than if they didn't know at all?

*A:* Yeah, because if I got upset, then they'd be asking, 'Why?'

Louise, aged 12

But a number of other children were uncomfortable with their teachers trying to help. Offers of support and understanding from the teachers were quite frequently interpreted as unnecessary (and unwelcome) fuss.

Teachers were like, 'Ooh are you all right?' 'Well, yes, I'm fine thank you.' The teachers were like, 'If you need to go out of the classroom for anything, just go'. 'Errgh! I just want to be normal, thank you!' That was the most annoying thing.

Derek, aged 13

Other children simply did not want to talk to their teachers about it or use them for support.

Q: Do people like your teacher know?

A: My mum told my teachers but I didn't, like, speak to them about it. They didn't talk much. I knew Miss [name] knew, because she goes, 'Are you all right? Are you living with your dad still?' And so I knew my mum must have told her. But I didn't speak to her about it.

George, aged 10

A position taken by a number of the children was that teachers should know about the changes in family circumstances but should not 'interfere'. This reinforces the point made earlier about children's capacity to discriminate between the various responses they wanted from those they talked to, a point returned to in Chapter 6 when considering how children sought out sources of emotional support.

Q: Do you think that teachers should talk to children about that sort of thing or do you think they should leave it to the family?

A: I don't think that they should get involved too much. But they should know, yeah; in case someone's upset about it.

Michael, aged 13

It seemed that many teachers made a conscious effort not to interfere and only became directly involved when the children became upset. At times like this, children usually considered teachers to be a source of comfort and support.

I did cry once, in school. I cried a couple of times in school. And they asked me, 'What's the matter?' And they used to take me away and comfort me and everything like that. Especially my form tutor.

Ruth, aged 13

*A:*   Well, my mum told her actually.

*Q:*   Do you think that was a good idea?

*A:*   Yeah, because she was really helpful. She was just really, really comforting to my mum, and making me feel better.

Rachel, aged 10

Overall, the children involved appreciated most of the efforts teachers made to help. However, a number of the children felt that teachers themselves were unsure of what to do in the situation and some were aware of teachers' own difficulties in knowing how best to help.

She [mother] said, 'Anne might be upset in school' and we had, like, reading lessons and he asked me to read to him. But he asked me questions like, 'Have you seen your dad lately? How are you feeling about this?' Which was helpful, but again he didn't know what to say to me really because he thought, 'What if she gets really upset while I'm talking about it?'

Anne, aged 12

So far, we have been concerned with the way in which information about the child's altered circumstances is communicated in the early period following parental separation or divorce. With the passage of time, the news seemed to spread, almost by osmosis.

Then my mum told her friends, and they told their daughters, they told my friends.

Josie, aged 13

*Q:*   Do most people know about it now?

*A:*   Yeah 'cos she [best friend] told one of our friends. I told her you can tell one of your friends and that's it and then her friends told the rest. *(sighs)*

Gillian, aged 9

It was common also for siblings, who were often at the same school, to pass the information on to others.

Q: How do you think they found out?

A: I think mainly 'cos Tom [brother] went to the same school as me. And he talked to his friends. And they talked to other people and they talked to other people and it kind of passed down.

Damian, aged 10

Living in small villages where 'everyone knows each others' business' also facilitated the spread of information.

Q: Do most of your friends know that you don't see your dad anymore?

A: Probably. Yeah. It's only a small village and everybody knows everything about us. We know things about them.

Q: How do you think they found out?

A: Probably spread. Somebody probably heard us talking about it in town as it's gone on.

Gareth, aged 9

A number of the children felt that others had simply worked out for themselves what had happened. This may have been from cues such as behaviour changes or the child becoming upset in public or because friends had witnessed changes at the child's home.

Q: Has anybody found out?

A: Like all my friends did 'cos they all come over my house and my dad wasn't there.

Rhys, aged 10

Finally, some of the children reported their belief that their teachers had told other children, presumably so that they could be understanding of the child's situation.

Q: Did they all eventually find out?

A: Yeah, they did when they found out that I was leaving class, they asked the teacher, 'Why is David moving away?' ''Cos their parents have split up.' Presumably that meant divorced.

David, aged 11

## Discussion

The importance of a child's friends during the crisis of parental separation should not be underestimated. At a time when peers are a central part of their 'normal', everyday lives, children placed a high value on being able to confide in their closest friends. In doing so, children were careful where they placed their trust and particularly valued the opportunities to talk provided by those of their friends who had themselves experienced their parents' divorce. This helped children to give expression to their feelings in circumstances where they had a reasonable expectation that they would be taken seriously and understood. Talking to close friends, especially those whose parents had split up, also helped children see their feelings in a broader context. Such things as they were experiencing had happened to others too. Children could be reasonably confident too that their privacy would be respected and that the flow of information could be restricted or at least controlled.

This was important because children, like adults, needed time to adjust and to be able to put on and maintain the right public face when it came to discussing their private lives and personal feelings. The pace at which children reached the point where telling others was less of an issue varied considerably. It seems to us that children were helped to reach this point by those parents who had themselves explained to children what was happening and hindered by those parents who prohibited their children from talking to their friends.

Children knew what they were looking for in talking to others and they valued the support that they received. They did not often want their confidant to do anything. Just to listen. Some children, especially boys, had real difficulty in knowing *how* to talk to others about what was happening to them. This may well be why friends were so very important. Adults may too often have felt the need to take on the responsibility of actively responding to the child or have misinterpreted what children were sometimes struggling to articulate. Far too many adults think they already know what a child is trying to tell them before the words are out. Children did not particularly enjoy 'being made a fuss of' or otherwise being treated differently, especially by adults, including teachers. We have noted at several points how, in finding a new point of balance in their lives, children actively strove to re-create a sense of 'normality' and this reluctance to be treated differently may be a part of this.

Children's faith in their friends was generally fully justified and this forms quite a contrast to the failure of trust that occurred between many children and their parents (see Chapter 4). There were exceptions, however, and some children did have to put up with some cruel teasing. It should also be noted that some children, certainly at the point in the process of their parents' divorce when we spoke to them, did not want to 'tell others'. They were not ready or did not want to. It would be unwise to assume that everyone, irrespective of his or her age, would deal with the same situation in exactly the same way. Children are no more an homogeneous category than any other socially constructed group.

In talking about telling others, children tell us something about how they feel and what they need that has a bearing on the responses that we as parents or professionals might make at this time. We develop this point in Chapter 8.

## Chapter 4

# Parent–Child Relationships

We noted in the previous chapter the importance children place on their relationships with their friends, especially in the period immediately after the crisis of their parents' separation. Such relationships, as well as being reassuring and helpful in retaining a sense of 'life as normal', proved, in most cases, consistent and stable. This chapter considers what children had to say about changes in the pattern, nature and quality of their relationship with their parents.

Where relationships between the child and his or her parents had previously been positively regarded by the child, these could more easily survive the family breakdown, however challenging the associated difficulties might be. Ceri and her mother, with whom she lived, had a lot to deal with:

Q: And do you think that while John [mother's new partner] is around that you'll always have this relationship with your mum?

A: The thing is, I think John [new partner] has caused a lot of problems with the relationship, with my mum. But somehow, because we're so similar and because we're the nature that we are, we'd be conflicting about something else, if it wasn't John [new partner]. And I don't have a choice really. It is going to be the way it is. I can only let her make her own mistakes and therefore support her. I mean, she's got another baby on the way in a couple of months, that's his. And I don't see how she's going to cope with that. She's going to need me at her house basically. I mean, like I said, we'll always be conflicting, but I love her more than anything in the world and she adores me.

She's the best mum ever. Even though she makes loads of mistakes. She does her best though.

Q: Do you think it's a good relationship you have with your mother?

A: Oh yes. We have some horrible times but we do have a good relationship. 'Cos, I don't know, 'cos we love each other so much I suppose. And we've always got that.

Q: Is it like you say, you've got to have a good relationship to be able to do it?

A: Yeah.

Q: To be able to go down there and come back again. Without a problem?

A: Yeah.

Ceri, aged 15

Oliver, aged 13, expressed succinctly how his relationship with his mother had improved and, in so doing, also suggested its value to him:

We can just stand in the room and just be silent and feel completely comfortable about it.

Many children expressed the same appreciation of the calm that entered into their relationship with their parents once the conflict between the adults diminished. Tom, aged 14, told how he gets on better with his parents:

'Cos they're not like arguing and they're not getting in bad moods all the time.

Anna, aged 9, echoed this experience in describing how, after her father had moved out, her relationship with her mother improved:

Because when she was, when my dad was living here, and my mum was going through the divorce, when she was living here for a while, um, she got mad and upset and she used to shout at us a bit 'cos of what was going on. But it wasn't on purpose.

A diminution in the level of parental conflict can also lead to improvements in what previously had been less positive relationships with parents. For example, Matt, aged 14, described how his relationship with his father was 'not as bad' as it used to be because his father was no longer 'as grumpy' as he was when he was living at home.

Children attributed improvements in their relationships with their parents to other causes too, not least the fact that their parents were themselves happier as a result of the divorce. George, aged 10, reported how his relationship with his father was now 'better':

> 'Cos he's more happier than he was when he was living with us and that. He's happier and that is good. He is happier.

Sioned, aged 12, who reports having got on well with both of her parents before they separated, still appreciates the relative calmness that comes from the absence of continuing conflict and an improvement in her parents' relationship:

> Well, he's more happier and more cheerful and so I think they're better now 'cos they got a divorce. They both say that they're glad now because they're still friends now and they're getting along better and it's peaceful; more happy because they're not arguing.

Positive relationships with parents after separation are also a result of changes in the child, especially those that seem to flow from 'growing up'. Ceri, whose difficult circumstances we noted earlier, spoke for many of her peers when she observed with remarkable compassion:

> Maybe we've just grown up a bit. I know that they're [parents] both human, which means that I've had a lot of problems with them and I've seen a lot of things. Now they both cry in front of me and I've watched them both go through awful stuff and I come out of it knowing that my parents are two human beings who are capable of making mistakes and therefore I'm not inferior or/and wrong when I make mistakes.

Much younger children reported similar experiences of getting to know and understand their parents better as a consequence of their divorce.

Q: How do you get on with your mum now?

A: I'm a bit better with my mum now. Now I'm a lot bigger, I understand her more.

Q: What sort of things do you understand now?

A: The words that she says; the words that she talks about. Her work. That sort of thing.

> Tim, aged 10

Q: How do you get on with your dad since they split up?

A: A lot better; I suppose 'cos I didn't really know him before they got divorced.

> Ralph, aged 10

Children also reported that they made efforts themselves to ensure that good relationships were maintained between their parents and themselves, especially where time to be with their 'absent' parent was considered precious (see below for a further discussion on children's vocabulary of 'time'). Julie, aged 12, described how her relationship with her father had changed in these terms ('cuchie' is a dialect term for 'loving, affectionate, cuddly'):

> Now I'm more 'cuchie' towards him. I'm more... Now that he's not living at home. You tend to take it for granted a bit. They're both there; 'Hi Mum', 'Hi Dad' when you come in. Now, because he's not there any more, when I see him, I'm probably more...a bit closer, you know, to him.

Keith, aged 11, also used his time with his father purposefully:

> It's [relationship with father] better. I think it's better than it was. 'Cos, you know, once you haven't seen him for the week, you get to sit down and you talk to him more. And you're more closer. Whereas when he used to work...

Perhaps it is not surprising that those relationships which children described in less positive terms are mirror images of those described as good. They are characterised by a more negative affective content, a greater degree of unresolved conflict, less satisfactory interparental relationships and a distortion of parent–child relationships. Where children articulated the emotional quality of less satisfactory relationships with their parents, these were dominated by expressions of anger. Sometimes, this was located in themselves.

Q: How do you get on with your mum now?

A: It's changed a bit, like, 'cos I've got bigger and I'm more angry most of the time, shout at her. Other than that it's all right.

Q: Do you sometimes shout at your mum?

A: Not really. I just turn round. Well, yeah, I shout at my ma sometimes. I don't really want to, but I just...

*Matt, aged 14*

At other times, the origins of the anger were more clearly articulated, as was the case with Nick, whom we quoted at length in Chapter 2:

Q: You said in the beginning you became angrier, more aggressive. Do you think that was a result of your dad going?

A: Yeah 'cos before I used to be like, like I always used to be friendly and stuff but if someone like shouts stuff about me I... It's like I lose my temper with them.

Q: So you've had more fights?

A: Yeah.

Q: Why do you feel that was?

A: 'Cos I'm, like, taking my anger out on people I shouldn't – rather than my dad. I should be taking all my anger out on him.

Q: Have you ever taken your anger out on your dad?

A: Yeah. Once in football training when I didn't wanna see him. But he just turned up and I started to shout off stuff and pushed him away from me.

Q: What sort of things were you shouting at him?

A: 'Get away; get out of my life', and stuff. 'You've hurt me enough.'

*Nick, aged 12*

Such a strong emotion could be very strongly expressed:

Hell – I hated him! Couldn't stand him. It was just the fact that he didn't treat me right.

*Samantha, aged 13*

Children who were experiencing unhappy or strained relationships with one or other of their parents frequently reported the source of their anger to have been the breakdown of the trust that had previously existed between them. Tim, aged 10, who, as noted above, had come to a more mature appreciation of his mother's situation after the divorce, still held very negative views of his father for this reason:

A: Well, when he said he was going to get back together, he lied. He lied about everything. He said he was going to stay at home all his life! He lied. He lies. He's not...

Q: Does your dad tell lots of lies?

A: Loads.

Q: How do you feel about that?

A: I was angry at him.

Q: Why were you angry with him?

A: 'Cos I don't like people who lie; even if it's any person of my family.

For Joe, aged 8, the consequences of the 'lies' he felt he had been told seem likely to have a long-term effect on the nature of his relationship with his father:

A: Say, what I'd really like to say, 'Well, Dad, why did you break a promise? 'Cos for starters I thought I might trust you to keep a promise'. And he said, 'Well, I did'. And he basically lied to me. In that sense. He didn't, he said he'd keep a promise that you'll stay here with Mum. And you're...and you'll never leave her. And he said, 'No, I didn't'. And I said, 'You did'. It's all part of marriage you mustn't leave them. So...and he promised that he'd never leave her. So basically he's trying to keep a secret from me. Because I, I've never lied to him before. So why should he lie to me? Why couldn't you just say 'No' to Debbie [new partner]? And, um, and you could have just kept a promise and not broken it. Because you broke a promise to my mum. And I'm not going to let you know any of my secrets. Because you might break it. You broke the promise...

Q: Do you think you might ask your dad some of these questions when you get a bit older?

*A:* No. I don't really want to ask him at all because probably when I'm older, he won't want to see me. And probably I, and probably when I go to see him, he won't allow me in his door. Because I might have hurt his feelings. Maybe. And think that I don't like him any more. I don't know really...

Michael, aged 10, lost faith in his father whom he felt had broken a 'promise' not to get married again. This left Michael feeling:

Muddled, puzzled, confused; feeling I don't know where I am. I'm real, like, in space somewhere.

The language of 'promises' and 'lies' remains important to children and this is discussed in greater detail below in relation to children's use of the language of time.

Children's anger at their 'blameworthy' parent also took into account the perceived effects of their actions on the other parent, often the one with whom they were living.

*Q:* How do you feel about your dad now?

*A:* I dunno. I haven't forgiven him for what he's done to my mum. I never forgave him for that.

*Q:* Do you think you'll ever be able to?

*A:* Never.

*Q:* Have you still got any good thoughts about him?

*A:* No.

*Q:* None at all?

*A:* He's never been a father to me and my brother and sister. He never, ever like spent any time with us. He never helped us with our homework. It's always been my mum, my nan or my grampy.

*Q:* Do you think you'll ever, when you are a bit older, do you think you'll ever be able to get on with him?

*A:* I dunno. You can't tell where he'll be. He's all over the place.

*Q:* Do you think he'll stay in the area or do you think he'll go off somewhere else?

*A:* I dunno. I'm not sure where he'll go.

*Q:* Would it bother you where he went?

*A:* No.

Catherine, aged 12

Susan, aged 14, was similarly unable to forgive her mother for leaving the family home, even though for her the overt conflict had ended. Her relationship with her mother seemed to have altered irrevocably:

*A:* But if Mum said anything about my dad, I'd go up the wall with her. I mean, I don't know why, but I feel like that.

*Q:* Does she ever?

*A:* No, 'cos she wouldn't dare 'cos she knows what I would do. I wouldn't speak to her ever again. I know that seems a bit unfair but, I don't know, I'm not going to let her get away with stuff. But if my mum said anything about my dad, like my dad says something about my mum, I don't know what I would do.

*Q:* Well, that's fair enough, because you feel very protective towards your dad.

*A:* Yeah.

*Q:* 'Cos of what your mum did?

*A:* Yeah, that's right.

*Q:* Do you think you'll ever be able to forgive her for what she's done?

*A:* No. I would never. I don't feel so resentful anymore. But I'll never be able to forgive her completely for what she's done.

*Q:* Even when you're much older? Do you think?

*A:* No.

*Q:* Do you think there's anything that she could do that would help you to forgive her?

*A:* Not anymore. Before. When it first happened, yes. But not anymore.

*Q:* How do you think you get on with your mum now? Compared to when she was living here?

A: I don't know really, yeah. I don't get on with her very well. I don't, we don't have arguments every time we see each other, but it just isn't close anymore. I suppose it was close at one time. But I don't know really.

Q: But you think it's not as close as it was.

A: No. Nope.

Children could also resent the demands made by their absent parent, especially when this left the residential parent with additional burdens.

> Now my dad spends all his money on his wife's kids and my ma spends less money on herself trying to help us have clothes and everything so I do love my ma dearly.
>
> Matt, aged 14

> I don't like him [absent father]. 'Cos he cares about the other, my step-mum's children, better than us.
>
> Kate, aged 9

Sometimes, this resentment was felt even more directly. As Catherine, aged 12, has already indicated, her rejection of her father would seem to have its roots in her perception that he had already rejected her. Her comments capture the anger, the sense of betrayal, the sympathy for the resident parent, the resentment of her father's new partner, the deep personal hurt and the confusion of many of the children already quoted in this chapter. When asked if her father takes her out anymore, she replied:

A: He takes us nowhere.

Q: How do you feel about that?

A: Disgusting. He should take his children out places. My mum can't drive. So the car's there to take us anywhere. And he's like got a car and a van and he could take us anywhere he wants, but he chooses not to.

Q: Why do you think he does that?

A: Don't know. He'd rather go and see his lady friend.

Q: Is he still seeing her?

A: I'm not sure. He says that he's stopped seeing her. But he's a liar.

Q: So you don't know whether to believe him or not?

A: No. He lies so much he thinks he's telling the truth.

Q: If you could say to him anything you wanted, what would you say to him?

A: I'd ask him why he done it. And what did he think of us when he was going off with her?

Q: That's the question you'd like answered. Is there anything else you'd like to ask him?

A: Did he think of her kids, more than he thought of us?

Other children, such as Bryony, aged 12, and Jake, aged 13, expressed their feelings towards their absent parent more in terms of regret and loss than in terms of anger. First, Bryony:

Q: What about with your dad? Do you get on with him the same as you used to? Or has that changed?

A: That's changed a bit because I can't talk to him like I used to when they were married. I used to sometimes cuddle him. I don't anymore. I can't. I don't know why. I just don't.

Q: Would you like to be able to still?

A: Yeah.

and then Jake:

Q: It's obviously different in that he doesn't live with you any more. But is it different in any other ways?

A: Nope. I do miss him sometimes, when I'm out in the shed. 'Cos usually he's out in the shed, working on stuff, like that, and I'd go out there and help him and stuff.

Q: So sometimes when you're out there now, doing that sort of thing…

A: Yeah.

Q: You'd like him to be around for you?

A: When I start this gardening; when I grow my cactuses that I look after and stuff.

Q: Does he have a shed where he is living now? That you can work in together?

A: Umm. He's got one, but it's not as good as that one here. It hasn't got a workbench or anything. So when he gets the time, he'll clear it all out and then put a workbench in there and light. And then start getting to work and doing the stuff he used to do.

The regret at what has been lost can be mutual and poignantly expressed. Claire, aged 10, in reflecting on the time her father spends with her, told how:

Really, he's had to realise how much he's gonna, how much I loved him. And how much he loves me and he's sort of realised that now, so he sort of does it a bit more. And he sort of stays.

Rosie, aged 10, thought her:

Daddy likes Linda [new partner] more than me. The only thing I wish is that it would be over, that they'd come back together. But they won't.

And Joe, aged only 8 and quoted already in this chapter, expressed the hope and compassion of many other children when asked what more could have been done for him during and after his parents' separation:

A: They could probably make up. Then I could see Mum and Dad again more. And say they just became friends and come together again.

Q: So you'd like your mum and dad to become friends.

A: Yeah, 'cos it's getting more hard work for Mum. She's having to be Mum and Dad.

Q: So, do you mean you'd just like them to be friends? Or that you'd like them to be back together again?

A: I'd like them to be back together again. Because if they're just friends Mum still has to be the mum and the dad. So I'd really like them to go back together again.

Q: Do you think that will ever happen?

A: I don't know. It depends if they do become friends. But I really hope it does happen, in future.

Q: Do you think it would be better for you if they do become friends even if they didn't get back together again and they lived in different places?

A: Yeah. 'Cos we'll get to see Mum; we'll get to see Dad much more. We can see Diane [father's new partner] much more because then they'd become friends with Mum. It'd be much more better.

Q: So it would be better for you if they became friends.

A: Yeah.

Where conflict continues between the adults, children are sometimes made to carry what seem like very uncomfortable emotional burdens. Nick, aged 12, whom we have already quoted talking about his anger, remembering how his mother and grandmother had 'helped' him, told how:

They just used to sit me down and talk to me and they used to tell me 'What you really want to take your anger out on people for? Why can't you take it out on your dad?'

Claire's father, who, as we have seen earlier in this chapter, was beginning to realise how much he had lost in terms of his relationship with his 10-year-old daughter, provided her with access to a pony but there were conditions:

A: And he [person looking after the horse] looked back, because he wasn't supposed to tell my dad that I was there. Because if he found out, he'd say, 'Why did you take your mother up there? That's not fair, he's mine and yours'. But I wanted my mother to see him. And I've taken the next-door-but-one neighbour up, and her little boy.

Q: Has he said specifically that he doesn't want you to go up?

A: He's said, 'He's mine and yours; he's no one else's'. In other words, 'Don't take anyone up'. I made out to him that I didn't know the way up to there. Which I do. I've been going for about 14 weeks. And, umm, because I know the way now, I can take a lot more people up. And he offered to take my friends up, but I can't take my friends up with him. He'd just ask them a load of questions. Like where do you live? What's your 'phone number? Has Mum been going out with her new boyfriend long? And things like that. And I can't trust him in that way. Which I feel so unhappy about, 'cos I can't trust him.

Q: Would you like to be able to take your friends up there?

A: Yeah, I would, but I know I can't. He asked me, but I know he'll ask questions. And Sam [friend] said, 'I'm not coming, if he's going to ask me questions, because I don't want to get involved'.

Q: Has he done that before then? Has he tried to ask your friends questions?

A: I haven't let my friends come because I know that he'd do it. So I haven't given him the chance. But he's been ringing round people, telling them that Jason [mother's new partner] has been going out with my mother and things like that. And that they're horrible people, and he's left the house with nothing. But he doesn't tell them that he's left the house with £7000 in debt. He doesn't tell them that. And everyone has turned against my mother. Her next-door neighbours, which have moved now, they didn't like my mother.

Children are regularly used as conduits for information or as a means of communication between parents. Bill, aged 8, describes how stressful such a role can be:

A: Well, yeah. Whenever we come back from Dad's and we go to Anna's [father's new partner]. Mum will say, 'What did she have to say for herself?' I say, 'Nothing', she keeps talking about it. And she really says it. She hurts my feelings but... So I just keep it a secret.

Q: So your mum hurts your feelings when she asks questions about Anna [father's new partner]?

A: Yeah.

Q: So you don't tell her things now?

A: Yeah.

Q: That must be quite hard for you.

A: Yeah.

Q: Do you find your mum and dad say things about each other when you're with them?

A:  I've never heard them say anything about each other but I'm a bit
    worried about the future; they might do it.

Q:  What do you think they might say?

A:  Some quite naughty words.

Q:  But they haven't done it yet.

A:  No.

Q:  So they might not do it.

A:  But I'm still quite worried about it.

Samantha's (aged 13) experience produced possibly even greater anxiety:

A:  Well he come 'round and my mum said, um, 'They don't want to see
    you no more'. And then he said, 'Is it true?' I just looked at my mum
    and she said, 'You got to tell him'. And I did and I had to tell him
    'No, I don't want to see you no more' and he just...

Q:  How were you feeling?

A:  Scared. I was really scared. I was, like, behind my mum, like, 'I don't
    want to see you no more'. And then he flew off the handle and
    walked out the house and slammed the door.

Q:  When you say he flew off the handle?

A:  Went mad. 'Why don't you want to come and see me? I'm your
    father' and all this. And I was just there, 'Oh please don't, please
    don't hit me' or nothing like that. And then he just walked out.

For Catherine, aged 12, the consequences of her father not yet having left
the family home seem likely to cast just as long a shadow:

A:  He, he just like, he don't leave us alone. Like he just won't go and
    let us get on with our lives.

Q:  Do you think he knows that?

A:  I dunno.

Q:  Do you talk to him much about it? Do you talk to him at all, when
    he is here?

A:  I don't want to be reminded of it.

Q: So you think, you'd like him to go, would you? And when do you think he will?

A: I'm not sure. Don't know with men.

Q: Do you think it will be soon or a long time?

A: Half and half. 'Cos he's got to go now. 'Cos he's got no choice.

Q: So do you think things are going to change much, once your dad goes?

A: Yeah.

Q: What do you think will happen?

A: Like, he won't be here all the time. We just won't have the worry of him. Just come here any time we want. I'll be OK once he's gone. Just while he's here, he pops up whenever he wants. He comes, sleeps here. I don't know why he's still here. He just does my head in.

Some children seem to have imposed upon them the entire responsibility for the failure of the marriage. Olie is aged 10:

Q: So, how did you feel when they split up?

A: I felt glad. But he kept on saying it was my fault all the time, so.

Q: Did he? Did he say that to you as well?

A: He said it was my fault because, umm, umm, I always used to break them up when they were going out somewhere. But I didn't.

Q: And that was what he said.

A: And he was always blaming it on me.

Q: And what did you think when he said that?

A: I felt upset.

Many children undertook emotional 'maintenance work' in support of their parents. For example, they answered the absent parent's anxious questions about the future.

*A:* But he'll frequently say, 'Do you love me?' 'You still love me don't you?' And I go, 'Yes'. And he'll ask me that every week. And I'm like, 'If I didn't love you I don't think I'd be coming here'. So it's a bit strange.

*Q:* Why do you think he asks?

*A:* I think because I live with my mum he thinks that she's going to take us away from him. And my mum applies for jobs all round the world, in really foreign countries. And he'll say, about my mum, 'I'll doubt if she'll get the job, or even the interview'. But he'll say things like, 'You will visit?' 'I'll miss you more than ever'. My mum hasn't even got the job! She hasn't even got an interview! And he'll say things like that, but I doubt my mum will move overseas.

Louise, aged 12

They also responded to their parents' regrets about the past.

*A:* He knew that he'd done wrong. He, um, told me sometimes he wished he'd never left.

*Q:* Does he still say that now?

*A:* Yeah.

*Q:* And how do you feel when he says that?

*A:* A bit mad really 'cos he just talks about things that I don't really want to talk about. 'Cos, like, when I said that he used to, like, go 'Guess what Richard?' and he used to go 'Oh, I love you' like that, and stuff like that and now like he goes 'Richard – do you love me?' and stuff and I goes 'I dunno 'cos of what you've done'.

*Q:* Does he still ask you that now?

*A:* Yeah, he still asks me now.

*Q:* Why do you think he asks?

*A:* To see, like, if I, like, trust him. He should and, like, he says 'I want to be as close as we were before'. I said, like, 'That can't happen because we're not living together'.

Richard, aged 12

Children also considered themselves to have a specific role in maintaining communication.

Q: Is there anything now, that you still need to do, to make yourself feel better? Or don't you feel the need anymore?

A: I don't think there's much need apart from to like keep my parents talking, like. To keep in touch. Then they can arrange days and that.

Daniel, aged 14

Sometimes they even assumed a responsibility for supporting a parent financially. Martin, aged 11, washed cars:

A: And if I earn, in about two days we'll probably do ten cars, so umm, we'll get £30 in two days, so that will be quite good. And that's the way I'm saving up my money, at the moment.

Q: You said that you'd given your mum some of that money. Why did you have to do that?

A: I didn't have to, I just wanted to.

Q: Was that recently?

A: No, but if I save up a lot of money, I usually want to give away some money if my mum hasn't got that much. She never asks for it. And I give it to her on my own decision. And if she does take some money, she pays me back and that.

Perhaps one of the most difficult situations that children have to manage is when they experience divided loyalties. This is particularly so in relation to contact visits (see Chapter 5 for a more extensive discussion of contact between children and their absent parent).

Q: How do you feel about the time you get to spend over at Daddy's house?

A: I enjoy it. And it goes like so quickly.

Q: How do you feel when you are about to go to visit your daddy?

A: Umm, well, I'm looking forward to seeing Daddy, but I really like miss Mummy.

Q: Do you feel that when you are going to see him as well? Do you feel that you'll miss Mummy?

*A:* Yeah. I'm looking forward to seeing Daddy.

*Q:* How do you think Mummy feels about it, when you are going to see Daddy?

*A:* She doesn't want us to go because she loves us and misses us *(laughs)*.

*Q:* Do you think she looks forward to you coming back?

*A:* Yeah.

*Q:* How do you feel then, when you are about to come home?

*A:* I can't wait to see Mummy and I'm going to miss Daddy.

*Q:* So it's the same, but the other way round, isn't it?

*A:* Yeah.

Emy, aged 10

*A:* But, you know, I'll have fights with Mum because of Dad and have fights with Dad because of Mum.

*Q:* Why would that happen?

*A:* I don't know, I mean…

*Q:* Is that if you are sticking up for one, or the other?

*A:* No, I never do stick up for one or the other. They can stand for themselves. Um, I do it with Mum the most because I just go and, you know, say 'I wanna, could I go over to Dad's a bit more often?' And she says 'I do try, you know, very hard'. Then it comes, somehow develops into a fight.

*Q:* What – and then you end up fighting with Mum because of it?

*A:* Yeah.

Shaun, aged 12

Joe, aged 8, was articulate in describing his own and other children's feelings, divided between his parents:

*A:* It's just that my friend, their mum and dad are divorced and they have one week with their dad and one week with their mum. So they sleep with their mum and dad one week. And, umm, we've mostly lived here and, umm, and when Dad suggested that we could sleep over there, Mum said that it was really hard to let go of us.

Q: Do you go and sleep over there now?

A: Well, we haven't really started yet.

Q: And you are going to?

A: Yeah, soon hopefully.

Q: Would you like to go and sleep there?

A: Well, if I really said it to Mum, she'd probably start crying. I would [like to] but I just keep it to myself.

Q: Why do you think your mum would cry?

A: Because she might think that I don't love her and that I just love Dad the most. So I don't really like to tell her that I'd really like to sleep over there.

Q: Do you tell your mum that you love her?

A: Yes.

Q: Do you think that she knows that you love her?

A: Yes.

Q: So do you not think that she might understand that you still love her, but you just like spending time with Dad?

A: Yeah, 'cos we usually spend the time with Mum. We don't really spend a lot of time with Dad.

Q: Do you think your dad would like you to go and stay over?

A: Um.

Q: So you think you might go and stay over there soon?

A: Yeah. Once we stay over there once he might invite us more. And when, if Dad says, 'Would you like to sleep over for three days?' And I say to Mum, 'Well, if he says that, probably next year', I'll say 'No', because Mum isn't ready for us to just sleep over there.

Q: Have you talked to your mum about that?

A: Well, yeah.

Q:   What did your mum say?

A:   Umm, well, 'OK then, if you have the nerve to do it, then do it'.
     And I said, 'I have the nerve to do it'. And if he says something, I
     know what to say, just say 'No'. Probably next year I might say 'Yes'.
     If Mum isn't ready, I'll still say 'No'.

Q:   Do you think your mum will be ready?

A:   I'm not quite sure because she likes things going nice and slowly,
     not speeding up fast. 'Cos she only expected us to go there once in
     a while. Then Dad came back, on the first time that we went there
     and he said, 'Can the boys sleep over at our place?' So it's all going
     fast. Too fast for Mum.

Not all of the children we spoke to were as articulate as Joe. That is not to
say that they did not possess feelings and opinions as strongly, rather that
they lacked the vocabulary to express them. One of the most striking ways
in which children, especially boys, talked about their relationships with
their parents following separation was through a vocabulary of time and
'doing things'. Expressions of loss were often mediated through a
metaphor of time and/or activities.

A:   Well, he always used to see me. I used to sit with him when he came
     in from work. Like, he used to take me places, go and watch stuff,
     cinema or go and watch football matches. And now he don't really
     take me to watch football matches. And he says like, 'Oh, 'phone me
     if you wanna see me'.

Q:   Does he 'phone you?

A:   Yeah. I 'phone him sometimes an' all.

                                                        David, aged 12

     No, we don't see more of him. 'Cos, like, where we used to live there's a
     field. After work, he'd come out and play football with us or something
     down the garden. But now we just go down the park, for a few hours.

                                                        Aaron, aged 12

A:   Well, I'm sad in a way, and only see Dad on weekends, you know,
     and sometimes there's not enough time to do what we planned. But
     then during the holidays I get to see him during the entire week.

Q: How do you think you get on with your dad, since the divorce? Is that better, or worse?

A: I don't get to spend so much time 'cos I don't really see him over the week. When we get the occasion we sit down and draw together, 'cos my dad likes drawing. So do I.

> Robert, aged 13

By the same token, time spent together was prized and seemed important in sustaining a positive view of the relationship a child had with a parent, even when other indicators suggested that the relationship with a particular parent was not all that the child might have wished it to be. Louise, aged 12, used time to convey much more about her relationship with her father than simply a detailed record of events:

Q: So how do you think you get on with your dad now?

A: It's better because when we did live with him, he'd come in, at about midnight sometimes, drunk, go to bed and leave at seven in the morning. And we're not even up.

Q: So, that would be his routine.

A: Yeah, or on a Sunday. What he'd do is, he'd come in early, seven o'clock, stay with us in the evening, complain all evening, go to sleep on the couch and then he'd go. He'd wake up in the morning and then he'd go to golf. And then he'd come up. 'Where's lunch?' And Mum would go, 'It's going to be about half an hour'. 'Oh!' He'd sit down and watch telly then have his lunch then sit down and watch the Grand Prix. Then I think he used to go out on certain nights to the pub. And that's when I think he saw Julie [father's girlfriend].

Q: Do you think you actually see more of him now?

A: A little bit, yeah. 'Cos I at least spend the day with him. And he doesn't just disappear off to the pub.

Q: You get the whole day?

A: Yeah. But when we did see… When we went for the week, he went to the pub, I think, twice.

Similarly, Nick, aged 12, still angry with his father, allocated time to him to reflect his feelings towards him:

A:  I still don't like him as much as I used to. He used to take me to football and everywhere but now he like takes me now and again.

Q:  Is that his choice or your choice?

A:  My choice.

Time spent together seemed to stand as a metaphor or symbol for the relationship between a child and parent, particularly his or her absent parent, and in the context of a perceived breach of trust on the part of one parent or other ('broken promises'), children did not easily accept excuses for being 'late' for an arranged meeting.

Q:  But he doesn't let you know beforehand that he's going to be late?

A:  No, *(laughs)* he just is late. He goes, 'Oh, yes, sorry, I fell asleep'. Like, half an hour later, and I'm wriggling, 'cos I'm supposed to be somewhere else.

Q:  Ah, so you 'phone him and say, 'Where are you?'

A:  Yeah. 'Where are you this time?' I always have a real moan at him. One time he was half an hour late, and I had to be at this dancing thing. Well, I was at dancing, and I had to go straight to the pantomime. He was half an hour late, and I'm in there half an hour late and I was already 45 minutes late!

Q:  And how do you feel about that?

A:  I was just shouting at him.

Q:  What does he do when you shout at him and tell him you're not happy?

A:  He says, 'I'm sorry, but I fell asleep!' *(laughs)*

Q:  Do you think that's a good reason for being late?

A:  No, pathetic. But he says he sets the alarm clock, but if the alarm clock can't wake him up, what can?

Q:  Is it because he has been working later, or something like that?

A:  Well, he works on nights, then he changes, but he has a weekend to get used to it. But he just goes out.

Q: So you don't think that's a good explanation, that he's working?

A: No, not that he's gone back to sleep. No, it's not, a pretty poor one really.

Q: But he doesn't change his ways? You tell him you're not happy with it, but it doesn't make a difference?

A: No, he says, 'But I'll be on time, the next time'.

Q: Do you believe that?

A: No. The following week he was quarter of an hour late.

Josie, aged 13

For children and adults lacking a complex emotional vocabulary, the 'facts' of time spent together was a very visible way of sustaining and managing their relationship, even if it could be a little forced sometimes. Some relationship maintenance tasks performed by parents might be understood as, usually appreciated, attempts to compensate for what has happened through the divorce. George, aged 10, believes that he now gets on better with his mother:

> I see more of her and she just, like, 'cos of the divorce, and she's trying to make up for all that, the arguing and all that. So I get on with her all right.

The situation was similar for Sean, aged 14:

Q: And so do you get more attention from your dad now than when he was living here?

A: Yeah.

Q: Why was that?

A: He was always at work and, er, he'd just sort of, he was always out and about and then we were, and, er, he just he, I don't know really. He sort of got in at sort of, seven o'clock at night. Saw him for like an hour, then went up and did my homework and went to bed and that was about it. And he was gone by the time I woke up in the morning. And that just happens every single day except the weekends.

Q: Whereas now...?

*A:*    We see him. Well, er… Well he, er, 'phones us all the time. He picks us up from things – he never used to. Um, he gives us more attention.

As well as sustaining, managing and taking care of relationships with their parents, some children had to negotiate a range of new step-relationships. Rarely were these introduced very skilfully to children. It would seem that many parents simply did not know how to tell their children that they had a new partner. Where they were not living with their children and the relationship with them was poor, a number simply kept it secret – even to the extent of not revealing that they had remarried.

> My dad got married. He got married without telling us. He didn't tell us for four months. So I was really upset about it, 'cos he didn't tell me. I said, 'Why didn't you tell me when you got married?' Then Trish [step-mum] bustling in, she said, 'Well, we weren't talking at the time. There was no point telling you'. 'Why didn't you invite us to your wedding?' Well, I wouldn't have gone, but I just felt like saying it. She said, 'Well, there was no point, was there, you wouldn't have wanted to come'.
>
> Cathy, aged 13

Resident parents sometimes sought to insinuate the new partner into the house – but children soon noticed when furniture and fittings began to change!

> My mum had a problem with her tummy and she went into hospital for a week. Mick [Mum's boyfriend] looked after us and at that point he told us what happened. He got together with my mum. Well, I thought, 'He's not my dad' and, 'Why is he here?' and suddenly all his furniture just moved in! He's moved his rug in here and he moved most of his china and things in the dining room. And it felt like, it just felt like, they were together and no one had asked me if he could move in or anything, he just moved in!
>
> Sarah, aged 8

Some children discovered for themselves that their parents had new relationships, largely through overhearing conversations or through their own observations. For others, discovery came as a shock, when parents introduced the new person in their lives after meeting them 'accidentally on purpose' while out with the children.

Mum didn't tell me that they were going out with each other at first. But what upset me a bit was that she didn't tell me. Mum was going out and she said she was going out with Mark [boyfriend] but she said she was just going out with him like a friend. Just a friend. I watched them go, walk up the road and then I saw them kiss when they thought they were out of range of the house.

Libby, aged 11

With Dad, it was just one day we were going into town and he said, 'Oh, you know your mother's met someone'. He started to say, 'And I can find someone else, you know. Well, I have'. And he said, 'We're going to meet them in town now. And then we're going to go swimming later' or something like that. And you're sort of, 'OK', and you're all sort of in one go, meeting them and going into town.

Rhiannon, aged 14

In such circumstances, children could feel extremely awkward and embarrassed. Much depended on the skill of all concerned in smoothing this over and enabling a new relationship between the child and the new partner to begin positively.

Claire [Dad's girlfriend] is really nice. We went to Alton Towers for the day not long ago. It was weird. Josh [her son] wanted to go in my dad's car. So then she looked at me and said, 'Oh, do you want to come in my car then?' I was like, 'Oh, OK!' So I went in her car. We were chatting then. We had a chance to talk more so it was quite nice. I felt comfortable then, anyway, 'cos she was really friendly and all that.

Julie, aged 12

Children appeared most comfortable when the introduction had been gradual and they had been able to become familiar with the new partner over a period of time.

We started off with Cathy [Dad's girlfriend] not being there; so we went over there for the afternoon and played on the computer and everything and, er, it sort of gradually built up to us meeting Cathy [Dad's girlfriend] as well.

Sean, aged 14

According to the children with whom we spoke, the single biggest influence on whether they and their parent's new partner 'got on' with each other was the degree to which the new partner attempted to act like another 'mum' or 'dad'. Where the children felt that this was the case, they were overwhelmingly hostile, regarding this as attempting to replace their own parent and assuming a role that the person was not entitled to play.

> It was a bit weird 'cos when we lived here, Mum started in this dating agency thing, she got a boyfriend, and he tried to be a dad to me. He tried to get me to do more things, like acting like a dad to me and I didn't like it. I told my mum that I don't like him. He moved in here and tried to change everything.
>
> Molly, aged 13

Children who described their parents' new partners as being like adult 'friends' expressed the most positive feelings about them. This may change over time, of course. For the majority of children with whom we spoke, new partners were a very recent event. It is possible that the 'friendship phase' represents a stage that relationships go through before they move into a more overt quasi-parental model. For example, Robert appears to be moving from viewing his mother's partner as a friend, to seeing him as a step-father:

> I get along with John [mother's partner] quite well and occasionally he can be strict, but I suppose it's just his way. He's used to it. He shouldn't change for me. I shouldn't have to change that much, I suppose. It's not like I treat him like a dad. I suppose I treat him like an adult that I know well, kind of like a friend, you know. I'm used to him now; and Mum, you know, kissing in front of me. Before, I used to think, 'Why in front of me?' You know. I understand now. If he had been my dad, that's how they'd be acting. I kind of think of him as that now, step-dad. I suppose I've got a bit used to it now, thinking about it.
>
> Robert, aged 13

However, in a small number of instances, where not only were the circumstances of the divorce acrimonious but where there were also continuing difficulties and a raised emotional temperature, children could remain implacably hostile to their parent's new partner. Most of the children we spoke to reflected on the advent of the new partner wistfully or with sadness. When asked how his relationship with his mother now stood, Robin, aged 8, said:

*A:*   There's only one adult.

*Q:*   Is it different in any other way?

*A:*   No, it's just different 'cos Mum's got a double bed and there's only one person in it. And I've got a side of my own up there.

*Q:*   Do you share with your mum sometimes?

*A:*   Sometimes.

*Q:*   How do you get on with your dad since they split up?

*A:*   Mm, all right.

*Q:*   Is it different from before?

*A:*   Yeah, there was two adults then.

Alice, aged 13, saw a deterioration in her relationship with her father now that he had a new partner:

> I think I'm not as close now. But I think that's because he's got a new family. I feel a bit left out.

A similar but more intense expression of such feelings could arise over the presence of new step-siblings. In this instance, Robin, aged 11, used the familiar metaphor of time to describe his relationship with his father and his father's new child:

*Q:*   How do you feel about the fact that your dad has already had another child and he's not married?

*A:*   Well, that's OK but the reason is that he's took interest of the other baby now. He don't care about me now.

*Q:*   Doesn't he?

*A:*   No. Doesn't spend any time with me, doesn't do any... When I was over my nan's, um, I was playing, and um, he just drove past Nan's house without dropping in and saying 'Hi Robin'! And there's one time when he took me to go play football. That's the only time he's spent with me since I've been going to my nan's.

Not that additions to the household were always seen negatively. There were numerous expressions of positive, if occasionally ambiguous, regard for the new partners of the resident parent. Michael, aged 10, skilfully used the metaphors of time and activities to describe his developing relationship with 'Jack':

A:  I might get a step-dad – Jack. I'm not fussed on Jack 'cos, um, like I'm starting to know Jack.

Q:  Is this your mum's boyfriend?

A:  Yeah. I've not told him about my hobby. I haven't told him about my Judo. I want to see more of him. We went on a walk and he was very nice.

Q:  So is he quite a new boyfriend?

A:  Yeah, he's very new. He was my mum's older friend, now he's her boyfriend.

Q:  How do you feel about that?

A:  I feel very happy.

Q:  Good.

A:  I mean, not to go to his house but, um, like my mum deserves somebody else. She's been slaving; work in this house, working hard for us. My dad, he's just been working with another woman.

There were also some positive expressions of regard for new siblings, despite the fact that it could be a…

A:  …bit more hectic round the house.

Q:  Extra people? But you get on with Sharon [mother], much the same as you always did?

A:  Like, she always tried to do fancy dinners for Jack and Vicky [new step-siblings] and cook the dinners and things like that.

Q:  It must be hectic when you're all here. How many?

A:  Six kids.

Q:  Six of you all in the same place. Do they sometimes all come down together?

A:  Yeah, they sometimes come down with friends, a friend. Sort out a room.

Q:  How many bedrooms have you got?

A: Well, we've all got one each. Molly [new baby] in a cot in Mum's room. And we've got one spare room downstairs. But they try to come down at different times so it's not too mad around here.

Q: Otherwise it would get a bit...

A: If they did we just get a mattress, like, if Vicky [step-sibling] came down, we'd get a mattress, put it down in my room and she could sleep in there.

Q: So do you like it when they all come down?

A: Yeah, it's nice.

Tom, aged 14

Whether the changes were welcome or not, many children had to learn to negotiate new ways of engaging with their parents as a result of the advent of their new partners. Rosie, aged 10, described her frustration at having to discover new ways of relating to her father when she visited him and his new partner (Helen):

Q: Do you enjoy going over there?

A: Yeah, but sometimes Helen can be annoying. 'Cos if I ask him for a bowl of ice cream or something, he says, 'No'. If I go in the kitchen to get a drink or something, and then say to myself, 'Dad won't let me have a bowl of ice cream'. Then Helen might be listening and she shouts out, without me knowing, 'Can Rosie have a bowl of ice cream?' And he says, 'Yes', to Helen. And I think, 'Why can't he just say yes to me, not to Helen?'

Q: In that situation, did you ask him if you could have a bowl of ice cream?

A: Yeah. If I say, 'Can I have a bowl of ice cream?', he says, 'No'. Go into the kitchen, talk to myself saying, 'I wish he'd let me have a bowl of ice cream'. And Helen might shout out, 'Can Rosie have a bowl of ice cream?' and he says, 'Yes'.

Q: So he says yes to her but not to you.

A: Um. He says 'Yes' to Helen and then 'No' to me, which I think is annoying because that might mean, 'Does he like me more than Helen?' And I'm his daughter. And sometimes, if Helen stops talking to my dad, I start talking and she starts talking over me. Dad says, 'Wait a minute'.

Q: To you?

A: Yeah. And I find that annoying, 'cos I was talking when she stopped. And he said, 'Stop talking, she was talking first'. She was talking first, but she had actually stopped. So that's annoying.

As well as being articulated through the metaphor of time, children's relationships with their parents (and others) were mediated directly through dialogue with them. Echoing a point made in Chapter 2, many children lacked a sophisticated 'emotional vocabulary' as well as a coherent 'explanation' for what had happened to them and this made talking about their feelings and their circumstances difficult. Moreover, many had fundamental obstacles to overcome when it came to talking to their parents, their fathers in particular.

A: But I can't tell my dad, but I tell my mum. So, like, I feel the same really, I feel a bit cross with him for leaving us and stuff.

Q: Do you ever tell him you feel a bit cross with him?

A: No.

Q: What do you do, if you feel cross with him?

A: Go up to my bedroom. Just be quiet and draw or something. Or cuddle into my teddy bears.

Q: But you wouldn't actually tell him?

A: No.

Q: Do you tell Mummy if you are cross with Daddy?

A: Sometimes or sometimes I keep it a secret.

Q: Would you like to be able to tell them?

A: No. Not really.

Q: It's one of those things you like to keep secret?

A: Yeah.

Emy, aged 10

*A:* But Dad just hates talking about anything to do with Mum, like; or Gran or anyone on Mum's side of the family.

*Q:* Has he ever talked to you about why that is?

*A:* No, I don't even think he particularly realises he does it. He does it automatically. Doesn't even think about it.

*Q:* Is he quite open to talking about other things? Or is he like that about a lot of things?

*A:* A lot of things.

*Q:* Would you like to be able to talk to your dad more about things?

*A:* Yeah, I think it's becoming more open a bit now, 'cos I can't stand up for myself in front of Dad. He's very, I don't know, manipulative I suppose and they have... I can speak to him a bit more now, but not, not about the things I'd like to be able to say to him. At home I'd able to say, 'Shut up!' or, 'Get out of my room!' Things like that, but I wouldn't dare say that to Dad 'cos I wouldn't know what he's going to say.

*Q:* Do you think as you get older that might change?

*A:* Yeah, I think so. I hope it'd change as I get older.

*Q:* You'll perhaps get a bit more confident too.

*A:* Yeah.

*Q:* Do you find that difficult, not being able to be open?

*A:* Yeah, yeah, 'cos you always have to cover your tracks and make sure you don't sort of spill by accident or something.

Rhiannon, aged 14

Where a child's relationship with his or her father was generally good, open communication was much easier to achieve. Ceri, aged 15, said:

I've a brilliant relationship with my dad, I love it. But I think I've got a better relationship with my dad than anyone I know. Definitely, yeah. We can go out together as friends and then we'll come in and he's my dad, but he really is my dad. He talks to me all the time and guides me. And doesn't just tell me what to do. He's just brilliant.

The importance of being able to talk to a parent, especially 'mum', was expressed by many children, as we have already noted (see Chapter 2):

Q: What about your mum? How do you get on with your mum now – better than before?

A: Better.

Q: Why's that?

A: 'Cos I can talk to her about things.

Gillian, aged 9

Q: If you were going to talk to someone about it who do you think you'd talk to?

A: My mum – that's the only one. She understands me very well. I wouldn't tell my dad nothing.

Michael, aged 10

Q: Do you get on better now or the same or worse?

A: Better.

Q: How?

A: 'Cos it's just me and my mum sometimes and I like speaking to my mum.

Rory, aged 12

Whilst children's greater preparedness to talk to their mothers is widely reported in the literature (see Butler and Williamson 1994), it is apparent even from those extracts reproduced here that the circumstances of the divorce greatly influence children's willingness and/or capacity to talk to their parents. It is mostly fathers who leave, thus reducing children's opportunities to talk to them and it is frequently fathers who are 'blamed'. It is mothers who stay, generally, and it is mothers who actually have the care of the child on a day-to-day basis. Even so, children did seem to talk more readily to their mothers. As Sioned, aged 12, said:

Me and my mum are very close, um, 'cos she always comforts me if I, for anything really. She's the one I go to for every problem.

Sometimes, neither parent nor child is able to talk. Like Emy and Rhiannon (above), Rosie, aged 10, and both of her parents have some way to go before they can talk openly to each other:

A:   But things that I don't want to talk about, like how I feel, I don't talk about. But…

Q:   Would you like to be able to talk about those things more?

A:   Yes. I suppose so.

Q:   What do you think stops you?

A:   I'm not sure.

Q:   Have you tried?

A:   A little bit. But sometimes Mum cries and sometimes I feel… I say, 'Dad, can I just talk to you?' And he tells me something and then he says, 'Yes, I'm just coming'. And I say, 'Oh, it's all right. It's nothing'. When really I want to. But I don't really feel as if I do. Because there's a funny feeling inside.

## Discussion

The quality of children's relationships with their parents after divorce is, in large part, related to the relationship that existed previously. Good, open and communicative relationships between parents and children seem able to withstand a great deal of internal and external stress. Indeed, once any divorce-contingent conflict subsides, relationships can even improve. Parents and children can come to know each other and themselves better and appreciate one another more.

In those situations where relationships between children and parents had, perhaps more typically, been less equitable and mutual, the stress of divorce seemed to have a marked negative effect. Children's accounts of these relationships were dominated by expressions of anger, usually directed at the 'blameworthy' or absent parent or simply expressed in the child's general view of the world. The failure of trust or the experience of 'rejection' that some children reported as a source of their anger was very commonly referred to by children who continued to experience less happy relationships with one or other of their parents. The language of 'promises' and 'lies', children's terms for the failure of trust that so often seemed to haunt both the divorce and the nature of subsequent relationships, remains important to children, especially when talking about whatever future contact arrangements are made. The loss and recovery of trust is important to children and seems to be a key determinant of their future relationships with parents.

Where conflict continues between the adults, children are sometimes made to carry what seem like very uncomfortable emotional burdens and some children seem to have imposed upon them the entire responsibility for the failure of the marriage. Some children became actively involved in managing their parents' conflict, through mediating information, for example. For other children, an additional relationship task they perform is that of 'looking after' the needs of one or other parent; answering the absent parent's questions about the future, for example, or responding to their regrets over the past. Many children experience 'divided loyalties' as particularly stressful. Where the emotional temperature of the parental relationship remains high and where parents themselves have not reached any kind of productive emotional resolution to the crisis, children's capacity for doing so is considerably diminished.

As in many instances they lack experience and a sophisticated emotional vocabulary, the language of 'time' (sometimes expressed in terms of time spent 'doing stuff') is often used by children as a metaphor or symbol for the nature and quality of the relationship between a child and a parent, particularly an absent parent. Parents and professionals should not underestimate the damage to relationships that is risked when excuses are offered for lateness or for failures to honour commitments, even the most ordinary (they might matter the most), that have been made to children.

Most children are able to negotiate the frustrations of forming relation-ships with parents' new partners, despite the fact that most parents seemed to have introduced them to their children very clumsily. Children appreciated openness and direct communication, although again in this chapter we note some of the obstacles to communication between parents and their children, especially between fathers and their sons. Children's sense of time is important here too. New relationships cannot be hurried and if an assumption is made that a new partner can pick up where a parent left off, this is likely to be met by anger and resentment from the child. In our view, children overwhelmingly revealed themselves to be flexible and 'philosophical' about their parents' new relationships. We were asking a little early in the process to discover very much about relationships with step-siblings, especially where these constituted a new household but we have no reason to doubt that the children we spoke to would continue to develop relationships with them in the same resilient and resourceful way.

*Chapter 5*

# *Contact*

Critical to the potential of relationships between children and parents during and immediately after parental separation are the arrangements they have for contact. The making of such arrangements, according to the children to whom we spoke, proved one of the most difficult aspects of the whole process of separation and divorce. Even when, on the surface, the family's relationships appeared to have reached equilibrium, contact arrangements retained a disruptive potential to reopen old wounds and tensions.

There is now an extensive international and interdisciplinary professional literature on the subject of contact between children and their divorced or separated parents which, taken as a whole, reveals a complex and sometimes conflicting picture about such matters as the circumstances where contact is deemed either detrimental or beneficial to children; how contact patterns change over time; and the differences between the ways parents and children, even within the same family, can view the matter. Although contact is widely believed to be beneficial for children and parents (see Rodgers and Pryor 1998 for review), there is substantial research evidence which highlights the difficulties involved in establishing workable arrangements with which all parties are happy (e.g. Cockett and Tripp 1994). Maintaining contact arrangements requires a considerable amount of negotiation between parents who are already experiencing difficulties in communication (Smart and Neale 1999). Furthermore, there are no clear roles or norms for post-divorce parenting (Seltzer 1991). It is therefore unsurprising that, in spite of parents' wishes for ongoing contact (Smart and Neale 1999), up to a third of children lose contact with their non-resident parent within the first few years of divorce (Cockett and Tripp 1994; Wallerstein and Kelly 1980).

There is clearly no prescription for successful contact. To date, there is little evidence on which to base evaluation of different types or frequencies of contact arrangements. Furthermore, few studies have used information from parents and children to determine what may be the best solutions for different families. In order to make confident assertions about what may constitute the most successful arrangements we need to know much more about the experience of establishing and maintaining contact arrange-ments from the perspective of all family members – particularly the children. In this chapter, we concentrate on how children are involved in the process of making and remaking arrangements for contact and describe children's role in the management of their newly ordered lives. Our main focus is on contact rather than residence as this was, for most of the children to whom we spoke, the 'live' issue but we will begin with a consideration of both and, in particular, focus on the critical events and processes that decided who was to live with and who was to see whom.

We described in Chapter 2 how parents and children recall quite differently the process of children 'finding out' about the separation. We noted there that whilst almost every parent reported telling their child what was happening, almost one third of children reported that neither parent had spoken to them directly. A similar divergence is apparent in relation to consultation over residence and contact. For the purposes of our study, we differentiated between 'residence' (the settled arrangements for where and with whom a child should live); 'seeing contact', which includes visits, outings, being picked up from school etc. but excludes overnight stays; and 'staying contact' which did involve sleeping over at the non-resident parent's house. We asked children and their resident parents whether the child had been consulted over arrangements for residence and/or contact (i.e. been directly asked) and also whether they believed the child had been able to exert any influence over the decision, irrespective of whether they had been consulted. We later looked to see what bearing being consulted or exerting influence had on children's level of satisfaction with the arrangements made.

Almost 6 out of 10 children (56%) reported that they were not consulted over the question of residence. Just over half (52%) reported that they were not consulted over 'seeing contact' and a slightly higher proportion of children (58%) reported that they were not consulted over 'staying contact' (see Figure 5.1). In contrast, over half of resident parents reported that they *had* consulted their child over residence (53%), nearly two thirds (65%) said that they had consulted their child over 'seeing contact'; slightly more (70%) reported that they had consulted their child in respect of 'staying contact' (see Figure 5.2).

**Child reports (n = 103)**

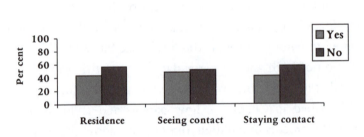

*Figure 5.1 Were children consulted over post-divorce arrangements? – child reports*

**Parent reports (n = 92)**

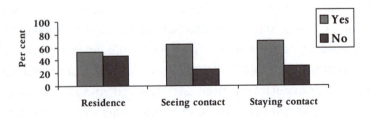

*Figure 5.2 Were children consulted over post-divorce arrangements? – parent reports*

A similar pattern emerges in relation to the degree of influence children and parents perceived the child to have over decisions about residence and contact (see Figures 5.3 and 5.4), although it is important to note that while parents reported a higher degree of influence by the child than children themselves reported (except in relation to residence), children did, generally, report more influence than one might have expected given the level of consultation that they believe took place. Indeed, over a third of children who reported that they had not been consulted over arrangements said that they had nevertheless exerted some influence over

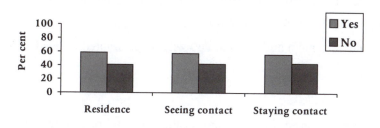

*Figure 5.3 Did children influence post-divorce arrangements? – child reports*

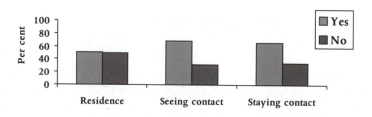

*Figure 5.4 Did children influence post-divorce arrangements? – parent reports*

decisions. There was a statistically significant correlation between the degree of consultation reported by children and parents and the subsequent influence the child felt over the critical decisions on residence and contact. For example, over 82 per cent of children who reported being consulted by either or both of their parents on the question of residence also reported having influenced the decision. Parents reported a very similar degree of influence following consultation on the same subject (80%). As one might expect, the child's age was a significant determinant of the degree of consultation and of the influence over residence and seeing contact that a child might claim for themselves or that a parent might claim for them.

Influence aside, it seems that children and young people are perhaps not consulted as widely as one might anticipate or as much as they would have wished. A number of children, especially the younger ones, recalled feeling excluded from this decision.

Q: Did your mum and dad ask you whom you wanted to live with?

A: No.

Q: Who decided?

A: Mum did, even though it was meant to be us. She just decided that we were going to live here. So we had to stay here. It was already decided that we had to live here.

*Joe, aged 8*

Q: Did anybody ask you whom YOU wanted to live with?

A: I wasn't asked.

Q: Who made the decision about what was going to happen?

A: I don't know really; nobody told me.

*Rachel, aged 9*

Mum just said that, 'We've decided for you to stay here the weekdays, so that we can get you off to school, 'cos your dad will be working and you will go and see your dad at the weekend'. I just had to go along with it really.

*Emma, aged 11*

Children were well aware of some of the practical constraints that operated around decisions concerning residence or contact.

> The decision was made anyway. Mum didn't have a full-time job, Dad did and he moved away from my school, so it was easiest for me to live with mum anyway.
>
> Libby, aged 13

Perhaps the most common pattern for consultation with a child was for parents first to make decisions and then ask their children what they thought of the proposed arrangements. This practice usually had the helpful effect of making the children (usually, the older children) feel that they had played a part in the decision-making process.

> Q: Were you asked what you thought should change?
>
> A: No. The only thing we were ever asked really was what we thought about it.
>
> Q: Were you asked what you thought when the changes were actually being made?
>
> A: Well, my mum asked me what I thought and then she said, 'How would you feel about it?' That was about it really.
>
> Helen, aged 15

As we have indicated, more children felt they had more say in decisions about contact and they felt they could change contact arrangements if they were unhappy with them.

> A: Well, my mum said it's difficult in the week, so like we see him at the weekend. But they weren't really arranged like, you've got to stay this long every week. It was just like he 'phones me and says 'Do you want to come round on Sunday?' and I say, 'Yeah'. He says, 'Well, if you come round at ten and then you can go home at six' or something.
>
> Q: Do you think what you wanted influenced the arrangements that were made?
>
> A: I think really it wasn't just them, it was us as well. To a point they were deciding more than us; like arranging things, but we did get a say in the arrangements. Like some days, I want to go and stay

with friends, but I have to go to my dad's, and in the end I just said to my dad, 'I've got to go and see friends as well'. Even if they ask me on a Sunday when I'm meant to be going to my dad's. It's just a case of changing the arrangements. It's a bit flexible so that you can have your own life as well.

Louise, aged 12

If it's on a day that I've got to do something or she says, 'Is it OK if I go out?' or if Dad says, 'Do you want to do this instead?' And she just asks me about it. And if I've got to do something that's quite important or I've got to go to a Festival and play my violin or that, she tells me to tell Dad, 'Could you arrange that for another date or something?' 'Cos she gets her diary. He asks me to ask her whether these dates would be OK, and she says whether it is or not.

Martin, aged 11

Notwithstanding these examples, there is an unambiguous message from the children to whom we spoke that they would have liked to have more say in decisions that affected their future.

A:   They just said, 'You're doing this' and, 'You're doing that' and I just kept to it.

Q:   Would you have liked to have been asked?

A:   Well, no point. I still don't think it would have changed their decision but I suppose I would have liked to have been heard.

Damian, aged 13

Children who were asked their opinions usually appreciated having been given the chance to have their say.

Q:   Were you glad that you were asked?

A:   I was glad that I was asked 'cos I thought, 'Yeah, I got an opinion'.

Daniel, aged 14

Despite most children clearly reporting the need to feel they had exercised some influence over arrangements, they usually accepted that the final decision was not theirs. More importantly, a number of children were keen to stress that they did not want to be left with what they perceived as the burden of taking the final decision. Particularly in relation to residence, several children described the difficulties they experienced when asked to decide who they wanted to live with. These children usually felt torn between wanting to have their say and not wanting to hurt their parents' feelings.

Q: Which was the hardest part?

A: When we had to say who we wanted to live with; that was the hardest part because at the time, I didn't want to hurt my dad's feelings or my mum's feelings. I never ended up saying who I wanted to live with 'cos I was so afraid I would hurt somebody's feelings.

Damian, aged 13

Q: How did you feel about being asked, and having to make that decision?

A: A little awkward really, you know, 'cos I just thought either way, one of them is going to be hurt, 'cos you can't live with both, if they're splitting up. So, I thought, 'Oh no!' It was awkward; I didn't really want to have to say.

Julie, aged 12

Most of all it was important to the children that they should at least be given an opportunity to prevent themselves from being forced into arrangements with which they were unhappy.

Q: Do you think you should have been asked whom you wanted to live with?

A: It would have been, well, not nice, but a good thing to be asked. Because if they'd asked, my parents, I know my dad would be saying, 'They've got to live with me' and my mum would be saying, 'They've got to live with me'. So, I knew if I was asked I'd say my mum. Still, I'd feel that I said it and they didn't make me live with one of them.

Louise, aged 12

Q: Did you think it was a good idea that your parents asked who you wanted to live with?

A: Yes, because they'd know exactly what I wanted; more of exactly what I wanted; not what they wanted.

Rachel, aged 10

The children reported a relatively low degree of satisfaction over the arrangements put in place for their contact with their non-resident parent. It seems to us that, in part, this can be attributed to the fact that at the time we were speaking to them, they were at a relatively early stage in post-divorce family life. Thus, the majority of children who talked about contact with their non-resident parent were still actively engaged in the complex process of attempting to negotiate and set up contact arrangements. The children described a wide variety of arrangements for seeing and spending time with their non-resident parent. Setting up contact involved having to juggle and negotiate a number of different elements to try to find workable arrangements that suited all parties.

Four out of five (85%) of the children had some degree of contact with their non-resident parent. Of the children who had no contact (15%), the majority came from families in which the separation had been between their birth mother and step-father (60%). All of these children lived with their mother and described step-fathers whom they had never liked and with whom they had no wish for contact. In all cases where there was no contact between the child and the non-resident parent, the children concerned attributed the lack of contact to poor relationships between themselves and their non-resident parent. Viv, aged 14, for example, had no contact with her father, and explained:

It doesn't really bother me that much to tell you the truth 'cos I never got on with him anyway really.

Of the children who had contact with their non-resident parent, the majority described their seeing and staying contact (74% and 54% respectively) as regular and predictable. Individual patterns of contact varied and ranged from very infrequent contact, to 50 per cent of time being spent with each parent. Other forms of contact, such as telephone contact, were common and particularly important for those children who had irregular contact, whose non-resident parent lived far away, or who were experiencing practical difficulties in maintaining contact visits.

Q: Do you ever get long periods of time where you don't see him?

A: There has been one or two weeks when I haven't seen him but I would still have heard from him. He always 'phones if he can't see me and there has been some periods of time when we go down the caravan, like, go for two weeks or a month, but I always 'phone him from the site 'cos we got a 'phone box.

Daniel, aged 14

In talking about their experiences of contact, the children described a wide variety of arrangements which took a great deal of management, much of which was apparently done by the children themselves, as we shall illustrate below. In talking to children about how they negotiated setting up and maintaining contact arrangements, children once more (see Chapter 4) used a vocabulary of 'time' as a metaphor for the emotional content of the processes in which they were involved. Note how Robert answers a direct question about the nature of his current relationship with his dad directly in terms of time:

A: Well, I'm sad in a way, and only see Dad on weekends, you know, and sometimes there's not enough time to do what we planned.

Q: How do you think you get on with your dad, since the divorce?

A: I don't get to spend so much time as I did 'cos I don't really see him over the week.

Robert, aged 13

The remaining children who did not report having less 'time' with their parents were almost equally divided between those who thought that their parents' separation had no effect on the amount of time spent with their non-resident parent (12%) and those who felt that they had more time with their non-resident parent (11%). By comparison, children generally reported less change in the amount of time they spent with resident parents. Indeed, just over half (52%) of them felt that they now spent more time with their resident parent than prior to the separation while 37 per cent saw no change and only 11 per cent felt they now spent less time with their non-resident parent (see Figure 5.5).

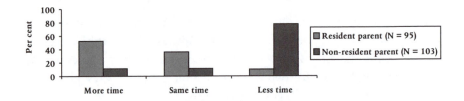

*Figure 5.5 Effect of separation on time spent with resident and non-resident parent*

As well as understanding 'time' in these terms, it is important to acknowledge that both children and parents were faced with a very real set of time problems to resolve. The children described the challenge they faced in trying to organise time with their non-resident parent along with the many other commitments that each party to the process had. Developing a regular pattern of contact arrangements meant having to arrange visits around parents' work, children's school hours, parents' and children's own social commitments as well as other family activities.

Q: Do you see your dad on a regular basis?

A: We used to but now both of us, me and my sister, we may be going out with friends or can't do it this night. It's not very often that the three of us can find one night when we are not doing anything.

Q: So, it's because you and Julia [sister] are busy with other things.

A: Yeah, it's not that we've given up on it or whatever.

Helen, aged 15

Although some children's social commitments were accommodated, most contact nonetheless occurred in children's own 'free time'. Indeed, contact often happened at weekends – time which was important for the children to spend with their friends. Having to share time between family and friends to accommodate contact posed a real dilemma for many children.

Q: Are you happy with the amount of time you get to see your dad or is there a better arrangement for you do you think?

A: I wouldn't like to see him every weekend because I, like, can stay over at friends' houses and see my friends a lot and friends are important to me. And I couldn't see him every other weekend because I wouldn't see my friends then. I don't know; I would like it to be more, but it really couldn't.

Q: What would be your ideal?

A: More half-term holidays so I could go down and see my dad. That would be it really.

Damian, aged 13

Time with friends was not an insignificant consideration for children, as we have indicated in Chapter 3 (and we will return to this issue in Chapter 6).

The question of time became particularly acute during 'high days and holidays' such as Christmas or birthdays. For many children it was important that they had contact with both parents on these special occasions but this was sometimes difficult due to the fact that time on special days was limited. As a result, many families had developed strategies for sharing time on such important occasions.

Q: What happens on special occasions like Christmas then?

A: Well, Mum and Dad have formed a sort of like Snakes and Ladders game and Dad gets us for one year, for Christmas, and then Mum gets us for one year. This year it's Mum's go.

Shaun, aged 12

Q: What about on your birthday?

A: Well, I know that I'll see my dad. It will be, like, I'll have my birthday party with my mum, 'cos my mum will organise that. When I go to my dad's, we'll have a mini-party; a family one, with cake and everything and loads of presents. But what he'll do is; my mum bought me some roller blades. Well, my dad paid for some of them and he goes, 'Mum paid for one boot, I paid for the other'.

Louise, aged 12

The management of contact was usually felt to be easier during school summer holidays. Extra or extended contact visits allowed children time with their non-resident parent without them having to compromise on other aspects of their lives. Children described the ease of being able to arrange visits and activities without the constraints imposed by everyday life such as early bed times or having to go to school the next day.

Children's views about the management of time also extended to the content of contact visits. Time was usually spent being in the house and doing 'everyday things' such as watching television and playing games.

> Just laze about in the house and stuff, maybe go out to the shops, DIY shops and stuff. Mostly helping him round the house and stuff like that, putting up new lights and stuff.
>
> Jake, aged 13

Or time was spent going out on 'trips', shopping or visiting grandparents.

> Yeah, he normally takes out quite a lot of money with him. We normally go to McDonald's or Burger King every week and we have dinner at Planet Kids. We sometimes go to the zoo.
>
> Caroline, aged 11

Some children felt that there was too much emphasis on activities on their visits. Children reported that they particularly valued time at their non-resident parent's home that was spent just doing 'normal' things. Special treats and activities were valued too but were sometimes seen as being compensatory.

> He was like taking us to the cinema. He was really spoiling us at first, quite a lot. He'd be taking us to adventure parks and things. Now he's got his own place, you know, everything has calmed down, which I'm glad about really because going out every week was like, not enough time to talk to my dad.
>
> Keith, aged 11

Overall, the children wanted 'fairness' in the arrangements made – both for themselves and for their parents. They felt it was important that they were allowed to spend equitable amounts of time with each parent and also that each parent had a fair share of time with their children. Keith continued:

Q: Are you happy with the arrangement?

A: Yeah, because that way it's fair as well. If we only go for one day then I'm still with my mum for the night; and then I'll spend some of the day with her.

Q: Do you think this arrangement works for everybody?

A: I dunno. I think my dad would like to see more of us. She [Mum] would like to see us as well. That's why, you know, it may be fair, but my dad says that we see our mum in the week. But then I have to say that, you know, I don't see much of her anyway 'cos I'm always out and sometimes my brother comes out with me.

Children's attempts at continuing meaningful relationships with each parent after they had separated were mediated by a number of other practical issues besides the simple availability of time. While parents were attempting to disengage from the marital relationship and begin to build a new life for themselves, the children were trying to develop individual relationships with each of their parents in a changing environment, often in a new location. As we have seen, the immediate aftermath of parental separation was a time of great uncertainty for many children. Children needed a great deal of reassurance that they would continue to see and spend time with their non-resident parent. Even with such reassurance, temporary living arrangements, parents moving long distances away from the family home, or feelings of upset, guilt or blame which surrounded the separation, meant that contact visits often took some time to establish. A number of children consequently had to live through an initial period of not seeing their non-resident parent.

A: For a while I didn't see my dad, I didn't have any 'phone calls or anything. I didn't see him for a while.

Q: Did you understand why that was happening?

A: I knew it was because my mum didn't want me to see him. I didn't think it was for any other reason. I didn't know if my dad would want to see me again.

Rachel, aged 10

Similarly, temporary or much smaller living accommodation sometimes meant that arranging overnight contact was difficult.

Q: Do you ever stay overnight?

A: No, he said there's no room. I could sleep on the floor, I could do in Leah's [step-sister] room – there's masses of space. I could sleep in Adam's [step-brother].

Q: Have you ever asked?

A: Yeah, we tried to. He said, 'No, there's not a lot of room to sleep in, only one of you can sleep'.

Q: How do you feel about that?

A: Fairly upset.

Michael, aged 10

Once contact visits were more established, children found themselves learning to live between two homes. Constantly having to pack and repack bags for visits was sometimes considered tiresome. In addition, some children did not like having their belongings divided between two homes. Inevitably, children often felt that they only had one real 'home' and that their other parent's house was somewhere they simply visited.

A: It's just a bit tedious having to pack for one night, school uniform and everything and have to pack clothes as well. It would be much easier if I had clothes at both houses.

Q: What do they think about the arrangements?

A: Rog [Dad] is all right about them, but they're not the most convenient of arrangements. Every other weekend, and half way through the week, having to pack my stuff and come back up again, 'cos its harder to get to school from Roger's 'cos it's further to walk.

Oliver, aged 13

I haven't particularly got my own room or anything. If I go down, I have to take my own clothes from the house and stuff like that. It's not the same, 'cos like here I can go to the kitchen, get myself a drink. I can eat in here [bedroom]. We have to go and 'ask' if you can have a drink; ask if you can have this or that, 'cos you feel as if it's not yours to relax in, sort of thing, it's different.

Rhiannon, aged 14

For some children, contact involved visiting a parent who had moved in with a new partner. Some children felt reluctant to visit in these circumstances because they did not want to be in the company of the new partner.

A: I never go round to his place, never ever been there. I'd never really want to with Tina [new partner] being there.

Q: Why's that?

A: 'Cos she's just so annoying. It's like, taking Dad away from me. I can't talk to Dad. Like, I can't talk to Mum when Martin's [new partner] is there and I can't talk to Dad when Tina [new partner] is there.

Q: When Dad comes to take you out, does Tina normally come, or does he come on his own?

A: He never comes on his own. We used to beg him to come without Tina. He used to say, 'No way'. 'Cos he'd rather be with her than us.

Q: Do you like spending time with him?

A: In a way, in a way not. He's my dad. I love my dad, but in a way, no 'cos he's with a girlfriend now and he's got a new life now.

Cathy, aged 13

Other children wanted to see their non-resident parent but were concerned about hurting their resident parent's feelings, as we saw in Chapter 4 when Joe described how his mother was not yet emotionally ready for him to spend more time with his father:

A: And if he says something, I know what to say, just say 'No'. Probably next year I might say 'Yes'. If Mum isn't ready, I'll still say 'No'.

Q: Do you think your mum will be ready?

*A:* I'm not quite sure because she likes things going nice and slowly, not speeding up fast. 'Cos she only expected us to go there once in a while. Then Dad came back, on the first time that we went there and he said, 'Can the boys sleep over at our place?' So it's all going fast. Too fast for Mum.

Joe, aged 8

Those children who shared their contact visits with siblings identified a number of issues resulting from having to share visits. Among sibling pairs it was common for them to want different amounts of contact with their non-resident parent. A number of children also described conflicts of interests between siblings who wanted to do different things on their visits. Children described either having to take it in turns to do the things that they liked or constantly having to do the same few things that appealed to everyone. Some of the children would have liked to have time alone with their non-resident parent.

*A:* Sometimes he might take us swimming, like once every six months or something like that. But if Josie [sister], when her mates see her, she doesn't mind not going anywhere, 'cos she can play with her friends but if no one's home [Josie says], 'I'm bored, I wanna go home, I'm bored, take me somewhere'. So it's like, it depends on what's going on.

*Q:* What things would you like to do?

*A:* I don't know. Sneyd Park was generally nice 'cos they got loads of half pipes and stuff for ramps for skates, I've been there a few times, but, stuff like that; just take us out a couple of times once a fortnight or that. It'd be quite nice. But if Josie's friends are in she says, 'No, I don't want to do that' and she'll just walk out the door. She makes a big fuss about these things.

Ted, aged 10

In learning to manage time, and negotiate arrangements around the practicalities of family members living in different households, the children demonstrated a remarkable willingness to compromise on their own needs in order to continue meaningful relationships with both of their parents. The children often gave up their own free time and were prepared to dedicate a great deal of effort to constantly moving and living between different houses. Even in situations in which the children felt that the arrangements were not 'ideal', many were willing to accept the constraints of trying to arrange contact around other commitments and activities and they were often quite happy with the compromise.

> Well, I kind of felt that it was a shame 'cos I'd only be seeing my dad on weekends but I'm glad I still get to see him. Some ones break up and never ever get to see the other one.
>
> Roger, aged 12

Where children felt they faced a greater challenge was in managing the range of emotions and feelings evoked from only ever spending part of their lives with each parent. Most of the children reported positive feelings about the anticipation of contact visits, particularly boys who looked forward to being able to share common interests and activities with their fathers.

> Q: Do you look forward to seeing your dad?
>
> A: Yeah, I always look forward to it, as we don't see him that much and it's fun when you go over. Play football and that.
>
> Q: What do you like best about visits to your dad's?
>
> A: Talking about football because, like, when you speak to your mum, she doesn't, like, have a clue about what I'm talking about, about football and that. And he does the things I like to do; like playing football, playing on the Playstation, watching car racing and that.
>
> George, aged 10

However, an inevitable price to pay for looking forward to and enjoying their visits was that a number of children reported feeling sad when they returned home.

> Q: How about when you come home?
>
> A: Um, Sunday, I don't know, I just feel like crying sometimes, you know. I mean, I know it's not going to do anything.
>
> Shaun, aged 12

The children's descriptions of their feelings about contact highlighted the emotional 'highs' and 'lows' that they experienced as a result of spending part of their lives with one parent and part with the other. While many children looked forward to and enjoyed contact with their non-resident parent they often, at the same time, missed their resident parent and other elements of 'normal' home life. Likewise, when at home with their resident parent, they missed their non-resident parent and looked forward to their next contact visit.

Q: How do you feel when you go and see your dad?

A: Happy. Sometimes I don't sleep in the night 'cos I know the next day is going to be with my dad.

Q: How do you feel when you come back again, after a visit?

A: I feel sometimes a bit upset because I think, 'Oh, I'm not going to see him again for a couple of days and now I've got all excited about it'.

Claire, aged 10

The children's adaptation to the repeated waves of emotion associated with contact varied (see Chapter 6 for a more detailed discussion of children's adaptation). Some children had managed to adjust to their feelings and the anticipated highs and lows had become part of their accepted new routine.

Q: How do you feel when you come home from your dad's?

A: Well, glad to see my mum again; sad to see my dad go but then I know that I've got the different things to adapt to, like, I can go on my Playstation. Whereas when I'm down my dad's, I've got to, like, kind of get down in the mornings 'cos we've got so much planned and I can watch TV up here and not worry about clashing with anything downstairs. Then I've got my comfortable bed!

Robert, aged 13

Others, however, clearly found managing the highs and lows more difficult.

Q: How do you feel if you're about to move from one home to the next home?

A: If I'm in one I miss the other 'cos then if I'm at the other, I'll miss the other one. I miss both of them really. Whether I'm here or I'm over at my mum's.

Maggie, aged 10

Q: How do you feel when you go up to see your dad?

A: A bit upset then 'cos I, like, love my mum. I'm quite upset then 'cos I miss my mum and stuff 'cos I'm quite close to my mum.

Q: Do you look forward to seeing your dad?

A: Yeah, but you know, I miss my mum quite a lot. Not there.

Q: How do you feel when you come back again?

A: Happy I suppose, I mean, I'm sad 'cos I miss my dad, but I'm not as sad as I am before I go. I miss my mum but I'm more used to living with my mum and stuff.

Damian, aged 13

For some children, dealing with contact visits also meant having to manage their parents' feelings. The children were often aware of the difficulties their parents were experiencing in trying to adjust to being essentially 'part-time' parents.

Q: How do you think your dad feels about it?

A: I think you can tell a bit that he doesn't want to leave either 'cos it's not just like a quick hug and kiss and goodbye, it's a tight squeeze. So you can tell a bit that he doesn't want to, like, leave but as I said, it's getting easier for him.

Julie, aged 12

As well as talking in detail about their own role in the management of contact in their family, the children also highlighted the impact of their parents' ongoing relationship with each other on their experience of contact. There was an overwhelming feeling amongst the children that it helped when parents could communicate and negotiate reasonably or were at least able to be civil to each other when making arrangements.

To make me feel better, I would like Mummy and Daddy to speak friends, to speak nice to each other. And every weekend, when Daddy knocks the door, I don't want Mummy to shout at him and say 'You're not having them'. Sometimes she closes the door on Daddy. If my mum doesn't open the door on Sunday, he won't pick us up, he just leaves straight away, turns back and he leaves and I don't want that to happen.

Lucy, aged 8

All too often, children found themselves becoming directly involved in issues related to their parents' continuing relationship. A number of children were still witnessing their parents arguing. This often occurred at the beginning and end of contact visits when parents met whilst picking up or dropping off their children.

Q: Do your mum and dad still get on?

A: No! Sometimes they argue at the pick-up point which upsets me 'cos I don't like to hear them arguing. Why can't they just drop it? It's like, they're divorced now. You know, it doesn't matter. Nobody owes anybody anything so I don't know why they ever bother.

Damian, aged 13

A: Mum and Dad argue a lot when they meet. Like about 'Who's going to take who?' and, 'What time do you want me to pick them up?' and 'I thought you said this but you said that'.

Q: What's that like for you when they do that?

A: I feel horrible actually. It's just I can't stop them 'cos one's my dad and one's my mum. It seems like it's all my fault when they're arguing. It just makes me feel horrible. I just feel that they're arguing 'cos of me, 'cos I was born and 'cos I have to be picked up at a certain time and it's just horrible.

Ellie, aged 10

Some parents' behaviour left their children feeling they were fighting to hold together positive parent–child relationships. This was often a difficult situation to manage. In some families children felt able to talk freely with their parents about time spent with the other parent. These children, on returning home from contact visits, usually began by talking through their visits and how they had spent time with their non-resident parent.

Q: Do you talk to your mum about the things that you do when you're with your dad?

A: Yeah, you know, if I've got a Sunday with my dad, I come back and she goes, 'Oh, what did you do today then?' And I said, 'Oh, you know, we went to bowling, we had a hamburger on the way back'. She goes, 'Oh, there's fun' and my dad does the same: 'What did you today?' 'Oh, we went to Merlin Park'.

Sioned, aged 12

However, this easy exchange was not always possible for some children. Stewart, for example, certainly felt that talking to his mum about what he had done with his dad might cause her to feel jealous.

Q: When you come home from your dad's, do you talk to your mum about the things that you've done while you've been over there?

A: No, not really, 'cos if it's a bit better, my mum might get a bit jealous, stuff like that. Like, if we come home and say, 'Oh, we've gone off to the cinema and we've seen all this', and she might get a bit bored of it and stuff like that.

Stewart, aged 9

Those children whose parents were unable to communicate reasonably, often reported having to take messages between their parents, usually concerning practical details about contact arrangements. When these messages involved simply passing information between their parents, the children were usually happy to do so, particularly when they felt they were helping their parents.

Q: Do you take messages, say, from your mum to your dad?

A: Yeah, like if my mum was at work today, like, she is until three, she would say to us before we left, 'Make sure you tell Dad to bring some clothes down before you come back over' or something.

Q: How do you feel about taking those sorts of messages?

A: OK, because it helps my mum and my dad.

Maggie, aged 10

A common feeling among the children we spoke to was that they were prepared to take messages between their parents in order to avoid any conflict that they thought would occur if their parents had to communicate directly with each other.

Q: When you are making arrangements do they speak to each other then?

A: No, they go through me or Craig [brother]. It'd be, 'Mum, is this time all right?' and we say it back to Dad, and things like that.

Q: Do you mind doing it like that?

A: No, it's easier in a way 'cos otherwise they'll always end up arguing on the 'phone so it's easier just to go through me or Craig.

Rhiannon, aged 14

However, the occasional instance of parents wanting their children to pass on 'bad' messages was experienced as very upsetting by the children:

A: If my dad's pissed off or something, he, like, tells me to say rude words to my mum and that. If they are talking over the divorce about something, my dad gets really annoyed.

Q: What did you do after that?

A: I didn't want to say something rude to my mum, but I just said what he said.

Martin, aged 11

Many children had to witness their parents 'bad mouthing' each other and for most of them this was a very unpleasant experience.

Q: Do you find that your mum and dad say things about each other?

A: I was with my dad and I said, 'Do you believe in aliens?' He said, 'I didn't, but I do now 'cos I was married to one'. I said, 'I just don't believe you said that' and I said, 'Mum doesn't say things like that'. I feel like saying, 'Mum doesn't say things like that about you', but I know if I said that he wouldn't really respond or anything.

Claire, aged 10

Despite finding their parents' negative comments about each other upsetting, some of the older children were still able to understand why their parents acted in such a way.

Q: How do you feel about that?

A: I kinda find it upsetting that the only way they can take it out is with silly little jokes. But I suppose it's the best way to get it out of their system than take it out on anger.

Robert, aged 13

Children also found themselves having to cope with one parent asking questions about the other parent's life. When the questions concerned practical issues, and the children felt they could be of help by answering, they were usually happy to do so. However, a number of children had experienced their parents asking for more personal information. The children usually found this situation uncomfortable and difficult to manage.

Q: You mentioned earlier that your dad asks lots of questions, about your mum's life.

A: Yeah, but I never tell him. He'll say something like, 'Where was she last night, 'cos I didn't speak to her on the 'phone'. I'll say, 'She was mowing the lawn'. He'll say, 'Are you sure?' 'Yes.' 'Are you sure she didn't go out?' 'No, she didn't.' 'If she did, who was she out with?' I go, 'No, she wasn't, she was mowing the lawn'. And she'd be mowing the lawn and he wouldn't believe it! But she is.

Louise, aged 12

Finally, in some cases, one parent had not wanted the other to know certain details about their new life and had asked their children to keep secrets. At other times the children themselves had felt that their parent might be upset if they knew certain things about the other and had decided to keep certain details secret. Whatever the situation, keeping secrets was practically and emotionally difficult for most children.

We tell her where we go on the weekend but we don't tell her any secrets that Daddy tells us to tell Mum which I won't tell her. Which I do but I said, 'Don't go up to Daddy, if I tell you' so I told my mum that she [Dad's new partner] was pregnant.

Lucy, aged 8

I didn't particularly talk about it with Dad, but with Mum for years she knew Mark [new partner], and we'd often go and see Mark, and whenever we came back, we'd go and see Dad and Dad would always ask, 'Oh, what have we done on the weekend?' We'd have to make things up to say we hadn't seen Mark or anything like that, as he didn't know about Mark.

Rhiannon, aged 14

## Discussion

Setting up and negotiating contact arrangements between children and their non-resident parents, following parental separation, is clearly a very complex process. Establishing workable arrangements that can accommodate the changing circumstances and needs of all family members is not easy. Many of the children we spoke to were in the relatively early stages of negotiating and practising contact arrangements and, in most instances, children were just beginning to adjust to spending only part of their lives with each parent and most were 'trying out' a pattern of regular contact visits.

In the initial phase of working out contact arrangements, there was often a brief hiatus in contact between the children and their non-resident parent. This was usually attributed to practicalities (typically fathers having to find new accommodation) or unresolved emotional difficulties. In this initial period all members of the family – the children, the resident and non-resident parent, and sometimes other members of the family too, such as grandparents – suddenly had to face the reality of the parents' separation, however much it might have been anticipated. It is in this fluid and often emotionally inflamed period when family members may be in a state of crisis, experiencing an acute sense of loss, that parenting arrangements about contact (and non-contact) have to be worked out. As far as we can tell from what the children have told us, these arrangements were more often than not negotiated by the parents with less consultation than children would have wished and sometimes altered following renegotiation.

The children were involved, either directly or indirectly, in the management of contact at a number of levels. The desire for stability and 'normality' in their relationships with both parents, which children wanted to achieve, had to be managed against a range of practical issues. In isolation, the children considered none of these to be insurmountable, but as a whole, they required a great deal of negotiation and compromise. We were impressed by the extent to which the children were prepared to forgo their own preferences in order to facilitate arrangements. Their involvement in managing contact inevitably forced them to learn to manage time in ways, and to a degree, which children from 'intact families' seldom have to do. They had to do so in situations that could be highly charged emotionally. Moreover, they had to develop the capacity to weigh and balance a number of competing demands. It was noticeable that in their accounts of contact arrangements, many children used the language of time as a metaphor for other things, particularly if they lacked the perception and emotional vocabulary to describe the nature and quality of their family relationships and feelings in other ways – a problem which seemed to affect boys more than girls. The children were concerned about how much time they could spend with each parent and about competition with siblings and new partners for their parents' time (i.e. their attention).

Most children considered that the greatest task was that of having to deal with the emotions they experienced in only spending part of their lives with each of their parents. In addition, some retained an overriding concern to 'look after', in emotional terms, the needs of their parents. The balance children sought was hardest to achieve when they were drawn in to their parents' 'unfinished business'. Some children saw it as their role to be the messenger in order to prevent explosive confrontation. But most wished that their parents could at least 'speak as friends' when it came to matters concerning them.

## Chapter 6

# Change and Adaptation

So far, we have explored the roles taken by children in managing the process and immediate consequences of their parents' separation and divorce. We have already shown children to be active participants in the process and have made reference at several points to how children, particularly in the early stages, seek to regain some equilibrium and sense of 'normality' in their lives. Yet, despite this, children's post-divorce lives are almost always markedly different in several important respects from their lives before the divorce. The experience of such rapid and often radical change is inevitably stressful for many children, as it is for their parents.

Other studies besides our own have documented children's responses to the changes consequent upon divorce (Demo and Acock 1988; Hetherington, Cox and Cox 1985; Kelly 1993). Studies that have examined the consequences of divorce for the adjustment of children have attempted to identify those factors that mediate how children respond to the changing events involved in family breakdown. Those factors that have been most frequently studied are age, gender and a child's personality. Early studies suggested that younger children may be more affected by divorce as they are less able to understand what is happening, more likely to fear abandonment, and have less accessibility to support (e.g. Allison and Furstenberg 1989). More recent reviews, however, question such findings, recognising that age is often compounded with time since parental separation (e.g. Hetherington and Stanley-Hagan 1999; Rodgers and Pryor 1998). Previous studies have also reported that boys may be more vulnerable to the effects of divorce than girls (e.g. Hetherington *et al.* 1985). However, Rodgers and Pryor (1998) also raise doubt about this finding as they conclude that interactions between gender and other factors make it difficult to isolate clear differences in outcome based solely on gender.

There is no doubt that individual children vary greatly in their reactions to parental divorce, as we and others have shown. Research has already highlighted that pre-existing emotional problems can be aggravated by the stress associated with divorce (Block, Block and Gjerde 1989). Hetherington (1989) reported that children who are intelligent, have high self-esteem and a good sense of humour are more likely to adapt well to the challenges posed by stressful life experiences. In a review of the adjustment of children with divorced parents, Hetherington and Stanley-Hagan (1999 p.133) conclude:

> There can be great diversity in the responses of children to divorce. Depending on the interaction of individual characteristics of the child and pre- and post-divorce experiences, new problems may emerge, old ones may be exacerbated or attenuated, or children's adjustment enhanced by their parent's marital dissolution.

However, to date, the majority of research that has attempted to understand how different children respond to their parents' divorce has been based on largely quantitative studies. As Jessop (1999 p.104) highlighted:

> Mainstream psychological and psychiatric research on divorce has tended to concentrate on the quantitative assessment of psychological states to the neglect of any understanding of the processes and personal meanings involved.

In this chapter, we explore directly with children how they accommodated the various changes taking place in their lives, what coping strategies they employed to manage change and how they felt they adapted to their altered circumstances. Here the term 'adaptation' is used to refer to the child's adjustment to the changes occurring in their life and the sense of psychological and behavioural balance that they were able to achieve.

The children we spoke to confirmed that the time of their parents' separation was a period of major and often quite rapid change. At this stage, as we have seen, most children felt a great deal of uncertainty about the future and were preoccupied with concerns about what would happen to them and other members of their family.

> I thought, 'Oh! It's going to all change. We might have to move'. I thought my father was going to be living miles away; I thought I'll never be able to see him again.
>
> Daniel, aged 14

At this stage, the children also feared the loss of friends and the possibility of having to leave their school.

> Q: What did you think was going to happen?
>
> A: We might have to move house and school, and live really far away. I was afraid that we wouldn't even live in England.
>
> Q: How did you feel about that?
>
> A: Quite upset and quite worried.
>
> Joe, aged 8

In the event, the most clearly discernible changes to the children's lives appeared in terms of their new 'time maps' and having to accommodate to belonging to two households, both of which were 'new' in the sense that each had household rules, domestic arrangements and patterns of expectation that were unfamiliar. However, while many children said that the practical aspects of family change became absorbed into everyday life, having to deal with changes that occurred in their relationships with their parents posed a greater challenge. For the majority of children the most significant changes that occurred during the process of family reorganisation occurred in their personal relationships with their parents (a theme that we explored in some detail in Chapter 4).

> I don't think it has sort of like affected me in regular activities, like getting dressed in the morning. But the thing it has affected me in is I just can't get used to seeing my dad on his own and then seeing my mum on her own. I'm just used to seeing them together.
>
> Jonathan, aged 12

Talking to children about their experiences of change following their parents' separation highlighted the extent to which the children valued continuity at the time of the initial crisis of separation. For many children it was critical that as much as possible remained the same in their day-to-day lives. We have already seen the importance of friends in children's immediate reactions to finding out about their parents' separation or divorce (see Chapter 2). Remaining at the same school and keeping regular contact with existing friends was particularly important for the children's accessibility to support from their friends.

> My mother said she wanted to move, but I said, 'Mum, if you move it's not going to be fair on me, because I'm not going to have any friends, I'd move school and I've got exams coming up now'. If I'd have moved, I wouldn't know any work that they'd done there, and I'd have to start all over again, and I said, 'Mum, that's not fair'.
>
> Claire, aged 10

Where little continuity could be maintained, the uncontrollable, and often unpredictable nature of change left children feeling confused and uncertain about their future.

> *A:* I think I was probably confused and, you know, I did wonder about the future. I was curious about the future, you know, what was going to be happening to us and what was going to be happening with Dad and things like that.
>
> *Q:* Did you have any thoughts about what might happen?
>
> *A:* Well, I thought bad things. I could just imagine Dad being really really lonely all by himself all the time.
>
> Will, aged 14

In addition, some children often still had to deal with ongoing conflict between their parents, as well as their own emotional reactions to the separation. Many children reported overwhelming feelings of confusion and uncertainty and most described frequent periods of sadness and/or anger.

> I was angry! Very angry with my mum and dad. But I didn't really like, take my anger out on them. I just felt it inside, that I was annoyed with them because they got a divorce.
>
> Sioned, aged 12

In response to the varying degrees of controlled and uncontrolled change occurring in their lives, children developed an equally wide range of coping mechanisms and support strategies. Here we use the term 'coping' to refer to the children's own management of their experiences. This definition includes psychological and physiological responses or actions that the children used in attempts to deal with difficult times throughout the divorce process. The term 'support' is used to refer to the help that children sought from others around them.

We found that children were remarkably active and creative in the methods they employed to cope with difficult times. Most notably, children demonstrated an impressive capacity for drawing on the resources of others around them for help. Just under half of the children (45%) said that they had sought support from other people during the divorce process, and of those who had sought support all but two said they had been successful in finding it. The children actively sought others to talk to in order to secure reassurance or advice, to spend time with as a means of distraction from what was happening at home, or simply to listen to them. Children were usually quite clear about what kind of help they needed and capable of choosing their confidant accordingly.

> Well if it's about the divorce, maybe something was troubling me, 'cos I really wanted to know something about it, then I'd go to Mum. If I was generally upset I'd speak to my nan or my best friend and maybe if I found something out about the divorce that really upset me, Sophie [friend] would probably come next 'cos she'd talk about it with me.
>
> Louise, aged 12

Parents were the most obvious actual or potential providers of support to children throughout the divorce process. Where parents' remained on reasonable terms with one another or where the children felt able to sustain separate and positive relationships with both parents, children often considered their parents as an accessible and useful source of emotional support, information and advice.

> Sometimes I'd talk to them about what could happen and whether this would happen and whether it wouldn't happen, or something. I usually talk to them and if I was sad I would usually cry on their shoulder or something.
>
> Matt, aged 14

In addition, children often chose to go to their parents when they needed physical comfort.

> When I was feeling sad and if I feel sad now, I can always have a cuddle with my mum and talk things through.
>
> Emma, aged 10

Children usually considered their resident parent best placed to provide them with support and a number of children regretted the more limited access they had to their non-resident parent, particularly boys with non-residential fathers. Will, for example, when asked whether there was anyone apart from his mother who could have helped him said:

A: Yeah, Dad, if I, sort of, saw him at that time, when I needed help but he, sort of, wasn't always there.

Q: He wasn't always there – can you explain that?

A: Well, like, if I was living with Mum and then I was upset that day – he wasn't going to be there but then again if I was, sort of, with Dad for the weekend and I was upset and he would be there but then again Mum wouldn't. So it was just who was there at the time.

> Will, aged 14

Not all children chose to go to their parents for help. Some children felt that their parents did not understand what they were experiencing and therefore could not help. Rosie, for example, felt that neither of her parents could understand what it was like for her and she felt unable to talk to them about what was troubling her:

Q: Do you think your mum and dad know what it's like for you?

A: It didn't happen to them, so I'm not sure. I think, sometimes if you're crying in front of them and they say, 'I know what it's like' you might say, 'No, you don't', because it's not happening to them and it hasn't happened to them. Then sometimes you think, 'How do they know what it's like, they're not me?'

Q: Have you talked to your dad much about it?

A: He just says, 'Oh well, there's no need to worry' and I think, 'Yes, there is'. It isn't just a few minutes of divorce; this is my whole life, so there is a need to worry about it. He says, 'If you want to say anything to me about what's happened', he says, 'do'. But I think, when something's wrong and I'm upset, I want to talk to someone, but I don't want to talk to him. Not because he fusses, but because I get a feeling inside that I don't really want to talk to him.

Rosie, aged 10

Other children recognised that their parents were too upset themselves about what was happening to be able to help. These children were often concerned about upsetting their parents further.

My mum, because she was upset, she didn't really talk to me much. She was always upset and I couldn't really say to her, 'I'm upset, I need a really good chat with you'.

Louise, aged 12

At the other end of the scale were a number of children who felt that their parents had 'moved on' and did not wish to be reminded of what had happened in the past. Cathy felt that her mother no longer wanted to talk with her about problems relating to the divorce, even though she still felt a need herself:

A: I don't know how she felt. She has someone to talk to about it now. We don't get a word in anymore.

Q: So you still feel the need to talk about it sometimes but you find it more difficult now to talk about it?

A: Well, it's sort of, it's really weird; 'cos, like, my mum's got a new boyfriend now and I don't think, I still haven't got over it yet; which I don't know if it's a bad thing or not.

Q: You don't really have anyone to talk to about it?

A:    My mum was talking to us. It's just up to us now. She doesn't seem to want to talk about it anymore. She's got a new life now and she doesn't want to talk about it.

Cathy, aged 13

Relatives were another valued source of support to children. Grandparents, in particular, were often considered as a trusted source of time, attention and reassurance especially during times of uncertainty. This was particularly valued by children who felt they were not getting the attention they needed from their parents who were themselves preoccupied in coping with their own stresses and concerns.

Q:    Is there anything anyone could do for you, to help you, as they get a divorce?

A:    I don't know. My aunties do and my nan.

Q:    How do they help?

A:    They help me by taking me over their house, by giving us tea and saying, 'Yes' to everything we ask.

Richard, aged 8

Grandparents' homes provided 'safe' or 'neutral' territory in which children could take refuge from what was happening. They provided a place where children felt 'at home' without some of the stresses they felt in their parental home(s). Grandparents provided the children with direct support, and the children also recognised that grandparents often played a role in supporting their parents (not least in practical ways) and felt that this took some of the pressure off the children themselves to provide such support.

Q:    If you wanted to talk about it at all, whom would you go to to talk about it?

A:    My nan.

Q:    Why would you go to your nan?

A:    Because she'd let me speak my mind and she'd let me say what I'd have to say.

Robin, aged 11

A minority of the children to whom we spoke had attempted to seek support from their siblings. Only one third (33%) said that they had talked about the divorce to their sibling and that it had helped. Children gave a number of reasons for why they did not feel that their siblings were a useful source of support. In some cases, the children simply felt that their siblings were too young to help.

Q: Have you ever talked to your little brother about it?

A: No. He wouldn't understand, 'cos he's too young.

Emy, aged 10

A few other children felt that their siblings were too close to the problem to be able to provide support. As they were experiencing the same problems, children felt that they would be unable to help them.

Q: Have you ever talked to your brother about it?

A: Not that I can think no, no.

Q: Why's that?

A: I dunno, 'cos he's probably got the same feelings so he won't help me.

Callum, aged 13

Siblings who did not routinely get on with each other seemed unlikely to forget their differences and turn to each other for support even when they recognised the potential benefits of doing so.

A: I talked to him a bit, but we get on really terribly; it's no use really.

Q: Does he feel that about you?

A: I don't know really, but he gets on my nerves a lot.

Q: So he's not someone you would go and talk to about it?

A: Definitely not.

Josie, aged 12

Another group of children identified differences in coping style as the reason they and their siblings felt unable to support each other. Some siblings inevitably coped with their parents' separation differently or over different periods of time.

Q: Did you speak to your brother?

A: No, we never. I would say to him, if he had anything, a problem with anything, or anything, that he could come to speak to me, but we wouldn't speak about it together. I think it was 'cos he didn't accept it.

Q: Have you spoken about it since?

A: No. If we sat down with Dad then maybe but we as siblings haven't spoken about it.

Sophie, aged 15

For most children, it was their friends who provided their most significant supportive relationships, especially for those children who found it difficult to draw support from parents.

Q: Who do you think was the most help?

A: My friends, 'cos I felt a bit embarrassed talking to my mum 'cos she was very upset as well so I felt she needed a break and it's not fair on her if I keep mentioning about the divorce so I went to my friends. So they were the most helpful, I think.

Sioned, aged 12

As well as using their friends as primary confidant following their parents' separation (see Chapter 3), children's peer relationships often provided their most accessible and trusted source of continuing support.

Q: Did you talk to anyone about it?

A: Just basically my best friends; basically the easiest people to talk to.

Robert, aged 13

Overall, more than two thirds of children said that they had talked to their best friend about the divorce and 86 per cent said it had helped to talk to them. Selected, close friends were represented as most likely to understand their perspective and the issues and concerns that the children had to deal with, especially if they too had experience of divorce. Friends were often also used by children to take their minds off what was happening at home.

Children frequently reported the value of being able to distract themselves by 'doing stuff' with friends.

Q: Was there anything that you might do that would make you feel better?

A: I'd maybe call a friend and ask them over to just do things to keep my mind off it. Like, I'd go into town and shop with them.

Louise, aged 12

More than half of the children said that they had no unrelated adult whom they felt able to talk to about what was happening. Of those children who said that they did have such an adult to talk to, half said it was one of their teachers; a few children had clearly found individual teachers helpful.

A: I talk to my teachers. Before, Mrs Wilson, she was my second teacher, but I found she was the most helpful.

Q: What did she do that was helpful?

A: 'Cos if I had any problems, about my mum and dad, she would always, like, talk to me.

Rachel, aged 10

The majority of children, however, were ambivalent about the support available from teachers. Most felt that while they did not necessarily want their teachers to become directly involved with their problems, it was nevertheless important that they knew what was happening so that they could take their circumstances into account should there be any changes in the young person's behaviour or schoolwork. It was important to the children that their teachers were understanding of their situation and offered a means of support even when they felt they did not want them to help directly.

I don't think teachers are good people to go to because they're not counsellors and they can't do anything. All they're good at is just teaching someone really. They help in a way but not really. It's just nice they know, in case, like, something happens at home and I come to school in a state or something. They don't know why, but they know something's going wrong at home.

Cathy, aged 13

(See Chapter 3 for a more detailed account of children's experience and expectations of their schools and teachers during the period of their parents' divorce.)

Few children had sought support from other professionals. Only one child had identified their counsellor as someone they could talk to about the divorce although some did comment positively on the support they received from 'ChildLine'.

Q: Was there anyone else who could have helped you?

A: Well I did ring ChildLine once and I had a word with them so that made me feel a lot happier. That was when they were first shouting. My teacher said it was a good idea to ring ChildLine and so I did when I was out in the town with my brother. I said, like, 'Oh, my mum and dad are always arguing and I don't know what to do and I'm really upset and nobody else's parents are like this' and she said, you know, 'Don't let this affect you and some parents don't get along with each other but it doesn't mean that they've stopped loving you'.

Sioned, aged 12

As well as seeking support from other people, some children found that spending time alone and drawing on their own resources were useful ways of coping. At times, children felt the need to release some of the emotional pressure they felt. Most reported the value of being able to cry about what had happened to them and many preferred to do this in private.

I go to my bedroom, have a good old cry and then, it's all out of your system and no one knows. I don't know really; speak to my nan and my dad. I didn't really speak to my friends that much about it. Like I'd never cry in front of my friends.

Susan, aged 14

Other forms of activity such as sport or play offered some children a useful means of venting their emotions safely although others used more aggressive or destructive means such as tantrums or causing (usually minor) damage to property. For other children, time alone for quiet reflection helped them think through what was happening. Some children, such as Claire, found writing down how she felt very useful. This helped her put her feelings into perspective and sometimes enabled her to reframe her experience in a more positive way.

> What I used to do is, I did have a little computer and I type things up and I save them. I do like a weekly diary of how I felt and what things had changed.
>
> Claire, aged 10

Some children coped by avoiding thinking about what was bothering them either by sheer effort of will or by escapist activities like watching television or sleeping. Others simply seemed to accept that things were as they were; they seemed resigned to living with their problems and adopted a 'keeping out of the way' strategy.

Only a few children described resorting to less adaptive coping responses. Typically, these children were often preoccupied with thoughts of what had happened; some resorted to 'magical thinking' as a means of coping.

> I still think it's all a dream and that it's all going to be better tomorrow.
>
> Rosie, aged 10

As well as drawing on their own resources and those of others to help them cope, children also reported being a source of emotional and practical support for their parents. This role often involved greater participation in household chores. Emotional support usually took the form of reassurance, especially for the resident parent; the age of the child was no predictor of the creativeness or genuineness of his or her efforts.

> I try to talk to my mother, like, if she gets upset, I tell her, like, 'Yeah, well, let's just get it sorted out' and things like that and she sort of perks up a bit, and then I just make her laugh about it. And say, 'Just you think how it's gonna be'. If things got better, like, if we were going to be million-aires, win the lottery and things like that. And I go, 'What would you do with a million pounds?' She went, 'I'd go and buy a villa in Menorca'. We used to go *(laughs)*, 'Yeah, in your dreams' and we used to laugh about it, and things like that and she sort of perks up a bit and so, yeah, we do help each other through it.
>
> Claire, aged 10

Some children came to regard the experience of living through and adapting to their parents' divorce as having some benefits. When reflecting on their experiences 'in the round', many of them felt they had become 'better people' as a result of their experiences. Some children felt they had become more grown up.

> I think I have changed. I used to be so much like Rhiannon [younger sister]. I've grown up now. I'm much more mature than I was before, and I haven't got a silly attitude anymore. I'm not saying I'm no more teenager, like, I still have my 'fits' and everything, you know, but in other ways I've grown up a lot.
>
> Susan, aged 14

> I think I've like matured a lot through it. I've had to make decisions for myself and stuff, just made me mature and more understanding of things.
>
> Nicky, aged 12

Other children felt that their experiences had given them a new perspective that helped them think about life in a different, and often more positive, light.

> I don't know 'cos I feel emotionally that all it's done is given me a different kind of view and slant on the way that I look at things and I think I've probably grown up quite a lot. I think I'm a better person.
>
> Ceri, aged 15

> It's sort of made me more sort of open-minded of how families work and things. It's made me realise, it's not all sort of get married, have kids, live like happily ever after. I don't think it's affected me in a bad way. It hasn't made me, like, go off the rails or whatever. I think it's just made me more open-minded about relationships and I think I understand more. Things like that.
>
> Helen, aged 15

A few children felt that they had gained in self-confidence.

> I improved in my schoolwork. I've become a better person. I've become more confident doing things. I've made more friends. I used to be scared to go off and meet other children; I'd just sit there and just listen to their conversation, but now I just go off and chat to anybody.
>
> Samantha, aged 14

When reflecting on all of the change that followed on from their parents' divorce, the children's messages were often positive. Whilst acknowledging how upsetting their experience had been, many nevertheless felt that things had worked out for the best.

Q: How are things now at home?

A: Fine really. My mum and my dad get on really well. Sort of just, come round whenever he feels. Fine really. Better now, I think, than it was when they were actually together. I think they get on a lot better. Now I suppose we make an effort to see each one of them. Fine really, no major problems or anything.

Helen, aged 15

Many children and young people talked with ease about their experiences and felt that despite living through what were inevitably difficult times, they had adjusted well to the changes and were returning to a new 'normality'. When we asked Will how he felt about the changes he had experienced he said:

A: Well, I knew I couldn't do anything about them so I just had to accept them, and then I probably didn't like them to start with but gradually got pretty used to them and then I don't feel there's anything wrong with them now at all. I think we've all got used to them and it's sort of just as though it's normal now. It's the changes that happened are normal now so if they change back they would, you know, be abnormal.

Q: Have you been asked about how you feel about them now?

A: Yeah, and I think I'll say, 'Oh, I'm pleased with the way it is at the moment, everything's fine'.

Will, aged 14

Q: How do you think things are now?

A: Normal really. It was different when Mummy and Daddy split up, but now, they're just like normal. I like it the way it is now, well, now that they've split up. When they get divorced it's not going to make any change 'cos they'll still love me and Matthew and they still won't love each other, and they'll still live in separate houses, and we'll still see our dad the same amount.

Emy, aged 10

We were also aware, however, that there was a minority of children who were not able to reflect on their experiences in such a positive way. These children were still experiencing a range of practical, emotional or relationship difficulties that were preventing them from moving forward and adjusting to their altered circumstances. One of these children, Shaun, was having particular difficulty coming to terms with his parents' separation. He was still experiencing a great deal of emotional distress relating to the divorce; this was usually triggered by contact visits:

Q: Do you still feel the need to cry sometimes, does it still get you?

A: A lot, yeah, I come up here [bedroom] and sit down and cry. Basically, I just sit down, try and read a book and go to sleep.

Q: Are there particular times when you feel like that, or does it suddenly come out of the blue?

A: Most of the time it's when we've come back from the weekends.

Shaun, aged 12

Similarly, Ruth was having great difficulty coming to terms with what had happened and was still experiencing a great deal of sadness:

Q: Do you think you're happy with the way things are now?

A: I still think it's all a dream and that it's all going to be better tomorrow, and that sometimes I wish, sometimes I feel strange but I feel I'm settling down with the arrangements now. But I'm still feeling really strange because sometimes I get really upset and I cry in my room because I think everything's gone. It's all gone away. I haven't got anything.

Ruth, aged 11

We wanted to try to understand fully what elements of the children's circumstances and experience might have contributed to their adjustment to the changes they faced following their parents' divorce. To help us do this we identified two groups of children in our study population[1] (see Table 6.1) – those who were having difficulty adapting and were still experiencing emotional distress relating to the divorce and those who had adapted well to the changes and who had achieved a degree of stability in their lives. We are not suggesting that the experience of parental divorce was the sole contributory factor in the patterns of adjustment we found. It is perfectly possible that patterns of adjustment reflect prior experiences or more enduring personality traits. The fact remains though that some children were coping better than others. There were some statistically significant differences between the two groups of children.[2] Briefly, those who had adjusted to their circumstances and experiences were:

- more likely to be a girl
- more likely to be older (aged over 12)
- more likely to have been told by a parent about the separation/divorce*
- more likely to have received an explanation of why their parents were separating/divorcing
- more likely to have found out about the divorce/separation early in the process*
- less likely to have kept the divorce a secret*
- more likely to have been consulted on residence/contact*
- more likely to have sought support from others*
- more likely to have received support from others*
- less likely to have received professional support (although the numbers here are very small)*
- more likely to have a best friend*
- more likely to have talked to their best friend about the divorce.*

| Table 6.1 Summary of data: adapting and less well-adapting children | | |
|---|---|---|
| VARIABLE | GROUP 1<br>Adapting children<br>% (N = 14) | GROUP 2<br>Less well-adapting children<br>% (N = 19) |
| **Gender of child** | | |
| Male | 43% (6) | 63% (12) |
| Female | 57% (8) | 37% (7) |
| **Age of child at interview** | | |
| Below 10 years | 29% (4) | 42% (8) |
| 10–12 years | 29% (4) | 37% (7) |
| Over 12 years | 43% (6) | 21% (4) |
| **Was child told about divorce?*** | | |
| Told | 86% (12) | 58% (11) |
| Not told | 14% (2) | 42% (8) |
| **Did someone explain about divorce?** | | |
| Yes | 50% (7) | 26% (5) |
| No | 50% (7) | 74% (14) |
| **When did you find out about divorce?** | | 1. |
| Immediately | 79% (11) | 39% (7) |
| During divorce | 7% (1) | 33% (6) |
| Decree absolute | 7% (1) | 11% (2) |
| Don't know | 7% (1) | 16% (3) |
| **Did you keep divorce a secret?*** | | 1. |
| Yes | 57% (8) | 67% (12) |
| No | 43% (6) | 33% (6) |

| | | | |
|---|---|---|---|
| Were you asked what should happen?* | | | 1. |
| Yes | 36% (5) | 11% (2) | |
| No | 57% (8) | 89% (16) | |
| Don't remember | 8% (1) | - | |
| Did you seek support?* | | | 2. |
| Yes | 43% (6) | 24% (4) | |
| No | 57% (8) | 77% (13) | |
| Were you successful in seeking support?* | | | 2. |
| Yes | 43% (6) | 18% (3) | |
| No | - | 6% (1) | |
| No support sought | 57% (8) | 77% (13) | |
| Did child have professional support?* | | | 1. |
| Yes | - | 22% (4) | |
| No | 100% (14) | 78% (14) | |
| Do you have a best friend?* | | | 1. |
| Yes | 100% (14) | 67% (12) | |
| No | - | 33% (6) | |
| Have you talked to your best friend?* | | | 1. |
| Yes | 64% (9) | 44% (8) | |
| No | 36% (5) | 22% (4) | |
| Not applicable | - | 33% (6) | |

*In some instances, where rounding has occurred, the percentages given may add up to more than 100.*

* *Those variables marked with an asterisk achieved statistical significance at p>.05.[2]*

1. *Data is missing for one child.*
2. *Data is missing for two children.*

By contrast, those in the less well-adjusted group were more likely to be boys and younger. They were three times less likely to have been told about their parents' divorce and twice as likely to have found out later in the process than their counterparts in the better adjusted group. They were more likely to have kept the divorce a secret and less likely to have been consulted on arrangements for residence and/or contact. Children in this group were half as likely to have sought support from others as their peers in the other group and less than half as likely to have received support where they did seek it. A third of the children in this group reported themselves as having no best friend and less than half of those who did, talked to them about the divorce. Children in this group also reported themselves to be less close to their siblings than those children who had adjusted better to their recent experiences.

We do not want to lose sight of the fact that each child's experience is unique and we do not want to imply that some kind of diagnostic or assessment checklist could be constructed from the differences we identified between those children who seemed more or less well adjusted. Therefore, we think it is helpful to re-examine some of the themes that we have identified earlier in this book in relation to children's adjustment and to reset their experiences in their own words.

The nature and quality of the ongoing relationship between parents after the separation/divorce would appear to be critical to children's capacity to adapt to the changes going on in their lives and to adjust to them. It was extremely important to the children that any conflict between their parents, which may have occurred prior to their separation, did not continue in their post-divorce relationship. Children who had adapted well to the family break-up more frequently described amicable ongoing relationships between their parents that were characterised by an absence of conflict and communication that was more open.

> I'm happy that they got divorced 'cos if they hadn't then they'd be arguing all my life and then I'd be all upset. And it's more happier, without shouting all the time. 'Cos if they haven't got divorced and I'm sure that they'd still be shouting now. My dad's happy and on the 'phone

now, my mum and dad get on. They're friends now. It's more fun and everything's happy – everywhere.

Sioned, aged 12

Not all children in this group had parents who had managed to achieve an amicable relationship. Parents of children in this group who had more acrimonious relationships were more likely simply to avoid each other and the inevitable conflict that would escalate if they met face to face.

The key role played by parents' ongoing relationships was echoed in the accounts of children who were having more difficulty adjusting. Children in this group more frequently described parents who were still in open conflict with each other many months after the initial separation. In addition, these children often became involved in their parents' disputes, either because the conflict occurred during change-over for contact visits or because the children were required to act as 'go-between' when parents had difficulty communicating directly with each other.

Q: Do your mum and dad still speak to each other?

A: No, never. They argue if they speak to each other. It's just, like, well you know, like, my dad's central heating's been broken this week, and he 'phoned and said that he won't be able to have us sleep over 'cos it will be too cold for us. Like, my mum says, 'Oh, but it's summer now'. So then just an argument goes on, and eventually the 'phone's just slammed down.

Keith, aged 11

Of particular importance were children's relationships with their non-resident parent. Examination of the accounts of children who appear to have adapted well suggested the existence of two quite distinct groups. Children in the first group describe relationships that did not change or only improved as a result of the separation. Typically, these children felt that they now spent more quality time with their non-resident parent than they did before the divorce. In contrast, children in the second group had no contact with their non-resident parent. All these children describe previously poor relationships with their non-resident parent that were characterised by fear or control. Children in this group were happy not to have further contact.

*A:* I was too scared. I was scared of him, anything he said I would do.

*Q:* Why were you scared of him?

*A:* Because of the way he treated my mum in arguments and all that and just scared of him. I told him face to face that I didn't want to see him no more and that was scary because he was in a bad mood.

*Q:* Do you think you'll ever see him again?

*A:* Hopefully not. I don't feel nothing for him. He's just a person who was in my life.

Samantha, aged 15

Almost all of the children who had not adapted well to their parents' divorce described generalised difficulties in their relationships with their non-resident parent. Many of these children had previously poor relationships with this parent that had only been made more difficult by the physical distance resulting from the separation. In a number of cases, the children described particular problems in the relationship that were a direct result of the marriage breakdown. For example, anger felt towards a non-resident parent for leaving and 'breaking up' the family.

General dissatisfaction with contact arrangements was more prevalent in the poorly adapted group of children, and usually stemmed from difficulties in sustaining already poor parent–child relationships at a distance. In addition, how arrangements were negotiated appeared to have some impact. Children in the well-adapted group more frequently reported open and flexible contact arrangements that took into account their other commitments and use of free time. Within these families, the easy and open negotiation of contact again seemed to reflect positive relationships and better communication both between parents and between parents and their children. In Sioned's family, for example, everybody had worked hard at maintaining positive relationships following the divorce. In combination with clear, negotiated and flexible contact arrangements, this meant that Sioned spent quality time with both her parents during the week and still had time for her own interests and activities:

> Like Monday we stay at my nan's in the evening, we stay the night up here. Tuesday, I stay at my dad's for tea and sleep there. Wednesday and

Thursday, here but my dad rings every day on those days. Then Friday I sleep at my dad's. Saturday I sleep at my dad's. Sunday, I sleep at my mum's. But sometimes, like, my dad goes away to see my gran and asks us if we'd like to come but if I can't – 'cos I do a lot of dancing, um, I just stay at my mum's and if Mum's got to go away for a couple of days with work then we stay at my dad's. So, it's OK – the arrangements.

Sioned, aged 12

We have already highlighted children's wish to be kept informed about what is happening generally and to be kept involved when decisions are made that affect their future. Analysis of the factors that mediated children's adjustment further suggested that adequate information-sharing and inclusion in decision-making helped children deal with the high levels of uncertainty experienced throughout the breakdown. Being kept informed about what was happening was a vital consideration to those children who had managed to restore some kind of balance to their lives after the initial shock of discovering that their parents were separating.

I was asked for my opinion on almost everything. What do you think we should do about this? Blah, blah, blah. How many times do you want to see Dad a week, and this, that and the other. You know, 'Are you OK if I move to this house?' and stuff. And yeah, I was consulted about most things and changes I did want to happen.

Oliver, aged 13

Those children who were having difficulty achieving such balance, in contrast, found that lack of information and exclusion made the task of adjusting to the changes in family life all the more difficult to achieve.

As far as support-seeking and other coping strategies are concerned, children in the well-adapted group frequently report available and effective support from at least one of their parents. In contrast, children in the poorly adapted group often make reference to a lack of support from their parents, either because of general communication problems or because parents were perceived as practically or emotionally unavailable to the children. Indeed, many children in the poorly adapted group reported that they were giving ongoing support to parents who were having difficulty coming to terms with their marriage breakdown. Very few children in the well-adapted group were still providing such support.

Q: Do you help your mum or your dad now?

A: Yeah, I helps my mum; comforts her; cuddles her; speaks to her and if she says, 'I'm fed up with things and everything', I says, 'Mum if you're fed up of it then just say to them you're fed up and you don't want it happening anymore'.

Charlie, aged 11

The importance of familial support in children's adjustment following parental separation also applied to other relatives. Children who adapted well often had large extended families that lived in close proximity and were thus available to provide support. In particular, the children in this group often had close relationships with their grandparents – relationships that were notably lacking in the children who had not adapted well. It is interesting to note that the use of professional support services only featured in the reports of children in the poorly adapted group, perhaps reflecting a general lack of, or ineffective, support from within the family.

Consistent with the accounts of children presented in Chapter 3 (and earlier in this chapter), which highlighted the central role played by children's friends following family breakdown, it was the support of friends that seemed to have the most direct impact on how well children adapted. Key factors identified in reports from well-adapted children included having close friends, with whom they felt able to talk and in whom they could trust and confide.

A: I like spending time with those people who are my two best friends. Judy is really nice and I can always go and talk to her and we always talk to each other if we have any problems and Gemma is really nice as well. Basically, it's just the three of us who are all best friends and we always hang around together.

Q: And what sorts of problems might you share with each other?

A: Um, boys – if they're annoying you. Um, basically, if you get told off at home – which isn't very often. Anything really, oh, especially she, Judy, really helped me when my mum and dad were going through the divorce.

Sioned, aged 11

Although some of the children who were experiencing difficulties adjusting had large friendship groups, many of these children nevertheless reported feeling that they had no one to talk to. These children were subsequently often left with many of their feelings 'bottled up'.

> I thought nobody needed to know except me. I didn't want Adam [friend] spreading it for me, so I just kept it bottled up.

> Michael, aged 10

The nature of children's friendship groups also appeared to influence the children's chosen coping mechanisms. The well-adapted children more frequently described spending time with friends as a means of coping during the divorce process. For many of these children simply having fun or being distracted from thinking about what was happening at home were useful ways of coping with difficult times.

> A:  If I, like, channelled my anger into something and if I talked to people about it, I found that helps.
>
> Q:  What things were you able to channel your anger into?
>
> A:  I did dancing at the time, I think. So, I was doing that. And then I started doing horse riding.
>
> Q:  Whom did you talk to most about it?
>
> A:  Mm, my friends, 'cos I wasn't really happy with talking to any of my family.

> Nicky, aged 12

The less well-adapted children, often lacking positive friendship groups, inevitably spent more time alone and resorted to more withdrawn behaviour and internalised coping mechanisms such as 'talking to teddies' or wishful thinking.

> Q:  So what would you do if you felt really angry, and you wanted it to go away?
>
> A:  I sit down and read a book; listen to some music; play a game; reading, 'cos I'm concentrating on taking my mind off things.
>
> Q:  What about if you're feeling sad. You talked about times when you feel like crying, what helps then?

*A:*   I just come to my room and lie down on my bed. Just thinking.

Shaun, aged 12

These children also tended to report more instances of bullying at school, often adding to their general state of unhappiness.

## Discussion

The findings of this chapter highlight the wide diversity of ways in which children experienced and adapted to change following their parents' divorce. Some children were clearly more resilient than others. They were more confident in their attitude to dealing with difficult times throughout the process and actively sought out others to spend time with, or to talk to in order to secure reassurance or advice or just to be listened to. Other children were more introverted and solitary by nature. They more often dealt with their emotional distress alone, sometimes through quiet reflection. Some of the children were fortunate in having plenty of support available from parents, other relatives, or friends while some had only a few people to turn to, and were left feeling isolated and unsupported.

Whatever the circumstances of the family breakdown, there were a number of factors that had a clear impact on how children experienced and adapted to the changes they encountered as a result of their parents' divorce. Those children whose parents managed to establish an effective parenting relationship, with an absence of ongoing conflict, seemed best placed to adapt to family change. Likewise, those children who were able to continue positive relationships with both of their parents, despite living in different places and sharing only part of their lives, had less difficulty coming to terms with their parents' marriage breakdown.

As we have seen, for many children parental separation came as a shock and resulted in a form of crisis in their lives. While they were attempting to regain some kind of psychological equilibrium it was apparent that being left out of discussions tended to increase the children's anxiety and upset. Dissatisfaction with inflexible or irregular contact arrangements, which exacerbated problems in ongoing parent–child relationships, also made the children's adjustment more difficult.

In their own accounts of what mediated their experience of parental divorce, the children consistently identified the overarching role of accessible and effective support. In general, children turned first to their closest friends, their mothers and grandparents for providing support. The key aspects of effective support identified by the children included support that they could access themselves, and at the time they felt they needed it, support that was strictly confidential and support that was provided by relatively young people who had some experience or personal understanding of the issues involved.

Alongside the complex interpersonal processes that accompanied their parents' separation, we need to remember that there was a series of external processes underway concerning the legal formalities of the divorce itself. It is to these that we now turn.

## Notes

1   The two groups of children were constructed on the basis of their scores on three standard measures: Achenbach 1991; Harter 1985; Kovacs 1981.

2   By convention, the difference between the two groups' scores was accepted as statistically significant when there was less than five per cent probability that this difference had occurred by chance.

Chapter 7

# Legal Aspects

In this chapter, we examine children and young people's knowledge, understanding and experience of the legal process of divorce. Many of the themes raised in this chapter are echoes of themes raised earlier, particularly in so far as they reflect the degree to which children are kept informed (or not) of the major events and decisions that are to affect significantly the future of their family life.[1]

Only five of the 104 children whom we interviewed had directly been the subject of legal proceedings. That is to say that in only five instances had parents made application to the courts to resolve residence or contact arrangements. Despite this lack of direct experience, almost three quarters (73%) of children understood that divorce was a legal process. For the most part, though, children had not been directly informed of any of the details concerning the legal formalities of divorce. Children and parents were agreed that little discussion on this subject had taken place between them. Seventy eight per cent of children said that they had not been told about the legal aspects of the divorce by their parents and 76 per cent of resident parents said that they had not spoken to their children on the subject.

Nonetheless, children made up for the lack of information supplied by parents and were resourceful in the number and variety of 'strategies' they adopted in building up their awareness and understanding of the formal process of divorce. However, some strategies led to misunderstandings, rather than a better understanding, of what was involved. For many, these misunderstandings heightened rather than lessened their concerns and worries, which, in turn, may have hampered their ability to deal with the crisis created by their family's breakdown.

Many children, especially younger ones, gleaned something of the formal process of divorce simply by observing their parents. From this, many picked up that divorce involved a lot of paperwork and letter-writing.

My mum's always writing letters to them [solicitors]. That's all I know.

Ryan, aged 10

Children also listened to adult conversations and telephone calls between their parents:

Q: How did you find out all about that side of things? Has someone explained it to you?

A: I find out when my mum talks to my gran and I'm around. I'm always listening. Things like that. And when my gran and my family use 'you know who', to talk about my dad, when I'm around, 'cos they know I listen. And I say, 'I know who that is'. Sometimes they say 'you know who' for someone else, and they use different voices for each person and I know which is which.

Jennifer, aged 9

Through overheard conversations children picked up some legal terminology, much of it outdated. However, this seldom provided them with an explanation of the term used or any understanding of what the underlying process involved.

Q: Do you know much about the legal side of divorce?

A: Not really, no. They haven't said anything. They don't tend to talk about that. I mean, Mum getting custody of us, that's all. I don't really know anything about it. They didn't tell me.

Jodie, aged 12

Some children 'worked things out for themselves'.

A: I know it is something to do with lawyers and everything, but I haven't really been told. I've had to suss it out for myself.

Q: How did you suss it out then?

*A:* Um, that, you know, that Mum was sending letters, you know I mean, sometimes I'd go and post the letters and read them.

*Q:* Who were the letters to?

*A:* To her lawyer.

*Q:* What sort of things did the letters say, can you remember?

*A:* No, I don't read the letters, just the addresses. But I did happen to come across one that said he hasn't been putting up, he didn't put up that much of the child's payments, for about, I don't know, four years, around there. And, um, so there was a long thing about that; a feud, if you like.

*Q:* Did anyone explain to you what was going on, in terms of the legal side?

*A:* Um, Mum did say Daddy hadn't been giving money to support us. That was all really. There wasn't any legal side or anything, you know.

Shaun, aged 12

Or, like Keith, others gathered information 'along the way':

*Q:* Did she [mother] explain what was going to happen?

*A:* Um, I don't think so, not really. I thought they had to go to court and everything. And she would have us, and that.

*Q:* Have you ever seen things about it on TV and that?

*A:* No.

*Q:* Just stuff you picked up along the way?

*A:* Well, just being there, when everything's happening. I've just found out.

Keith, aged 11

A small number had read books about divorce but most turned to television and films for information.

*Q:* How do you think you know about it?

A: Movies!

*Q:* Movies?!

A:    Yeah, *Mrs Doubtfire*. They had to go to court then.

Q:    Where else have you learnt about divorce?

A:    Mum's told me stuff and there's a couple of books in my school, in the library.

Scott, aged 9

Around the time most of the parents were separating, a number of popular soap operas were featuring story-lines focusing on family problems. These story-lines contributed considerably to how many of the children came to understand the legal process.

Q:    Tell me what you know about the legal side of divorce.

A:    Um, well, if you want to get a divorce, you can tell you want to get divorced and if you want to give grounds for, you can, and you get it done. But, most people just wait for two years. It was on *EastEnders*.[2]

Q:    Did someone tell you?

A:    No, I just knew.

Q:    Do you know what you have to do when you get divorced?

A:    You go to a solicitor's.

Q:    And what happens there?

A:    Um, both people go and see a solicitor or they go to the same one or different ones. And the solicitors call each other back and they put it through a legal basis and if people don't decide then they have an argument over who gets the kids. Or they decide, like Mum and Dad just decided. But some people have an argument over it and some people don't.

Q:    And what do you think happens if they argue about it?

A:    It goes to court.

Q:    And then what happens?

*A:* The judge decides. People put a case forward saying who we think is more suitable and stuff like that. Then the judge decides. That's on *Brookside*![3]

Ted, aged 10

Two major difficulties followed from gleaning information from media sources: first, 'the law' that the majority of children saw most of the time tended to focus on criminal cases which bore little relationship to the civil proceedings in which their parents were engaged. Second, the legal system portrayed was often that of the United States, not the United Kingdom. Not surprisingly, children reached conclusions that were at times unrealistic and, at others, simply wrong:

> Well, I've seen *Judge Judy*[4] on ITV. Have you seen that? They have things like that on. You know, go to court and everything. I don't know if it's the same over here. I've just never, I really don't know how it works. I've got no idea, to be honest.

Ceri, aged 15

*A:* I only know, like my dad told me. He was going to see a judge and we had to go with him. Which I didn't want to. My mum was going to see a court. And have my dad put down as guilty, but I don't want my dad to be guilty.

*Q:* Do you know what she was going to court for?

*A:* To get the divorce over and done with, and sorted out, all of the arguments.

*Q:* What do you think happens if you go to court?

*A:* It seems like Deirdre,[5] she was found guilty. I don't want my mum to be, or my dad to be guilty. But one of them has to be guilty, but I don't want none of them to be guilty. I felt scared, 'cos I thought we had to go with him and stand up in one of those boxes, if we were older, and say who we wanted to live with and who we wanted to put down as guilty or something. Now I'd say I don't want anyone to be guilty.

Lucy, aged 8

This quotation from Lucy reflects misunderstanding that many of the younger children had; first, that their parents might have to appear in court in front of a judge, and second, that, in legal terms, one of their divorcing parents must be found 'guilty'.

A:   The worst thing [about divorce] is when they actually go to court to see who has the children.

Q:   Do you know what happens if they go to court?

A:   No.

Q:   What do you think happens?

A:   They argue who wants to have the children.

Q:   Then who do you think decides?

A:   The judge. 'Cos I reckon they ask questions, who's been seeing the children more.

Q:   What do you think the judge does?

A:   He says who's going to have them.

Gary, aged 10

A:   I wasn't told. But Dad said something about they were going to court.

Q:   What did you think it meant?

A:   I thought that they were gonna get like, arrested, or like that, go to court.

Shaun, aged 10

Linked to these misunderstandings was a frequently held view that children themselves might have to appear in court. Like Lucy, many children, including older teenagers, found the prospect of having to go to court very unwelcome.

Q:   How would you have felt if you had to go to court?

A:   I think I wouldn't want to. People around and people you don't even know and that.

Q:   What do you think it would've been like?

*A:*    I don't know. The thing is, I only get an idea of what you'd have to do off the telly and things like that. The one I remember was on *Coronation Street* when I think it was when Gail's husband wanted to adopt Nicky or something like that. And he had to stand up in court and say 'yes' and 'no', and I thought it would be like that. Answering questions, 'Who would you like to live with?' 'Why?' Things like that.

Rachel, aged 13

Susan, along with others, feared appearing to be disloyal to one or other of their parents:

*A:*    [I thought]… we had to go to court but it never happened and I'm glad that it never happened. I didn't really want to go in front of my mum saying 'I want to live with my dad' in a court.

*Q:*   How did you feel that you might have to go to court?

*A:*    Frightened. 'Cos I've never been in a courtroom. Saying, in front of her, that you don't want to live with your mum. That would have been really bad. I'm not sure but I don't think the children have to go into the courtroom itself. They can go in a separate room. But I'm not really sure about anything.

Susan, aged 14

We have described, at various points (see, for example, Chapter 2), how children wanted their parents to provide them with much more information about their family's breakdown than was usually the case. However, children viewed the legal process somewhat differently. Partly driven by their misunderstandings perhaps (e.g. fears of a parent being found 'guilty'), most children believed the legal minutiae of divorce were 'confidential' and 'private' to their parents. Most accepted that the topic should be spoken of less often and that their parents might be reluctant to share any details with them.

*Q:*   Do you know anything about solicitors and lawyers?

*A:*    Yeah, my mum's always writing letters to them, that's all I know about them.

*Q:*   What do you think happens?

A:  Probably go to court and something like that but I wouldn't know, 'cos my mum just keeps that to herself.

George, aged 10

I know they got to go to the solicitors. But like, they don't tell me anything about it, because like, it would be boring. And like it's private and they probably won't. They won't tell each other, it'll just be like their secret.

Emy, aged 10

On occasions, the formal, legal process took place literally behind closed doors.

Q:  Did you ever meet any of the legal people, solicitors or people like that?

A:  I sat in the waiting room and saw the secretary. But then Mum just disappeared into a room. You try and peep through the door and they're gone. You couldn't go in there.

Q:  So, your mum and dad didn't go to court?

A:  No. No, they just, all done in private.

Louise, aged 12

Some children felt embarrassed to ask their parents about the legal aspects or to appear too interested in them. Again, these feelings were often coloured by the belief that such matters were 'private'.

A:  I remember going round to my dad's house and there was a 'home divorce kit'. And I thought, 'Oh my God!' It was kind of a little game or something.

Q:  Did you actually look at the kit?

A:  No. No, I didn't know whether I should or not; just pick it up and look at it.

Helen, aged 15

Other children sensed that their parents were choosing to keep detailed information (e.g. allegations of misconduct, adultery) from them to protect them from additional upset or worry.

All I really know about Mum and Dad's divorce is the money side. My dad didn't tell me about the divorce papers, 'cos I know there was a lot of things that Mum put on there which was quite cruel and untrue. Dad just told me a couple of things that were on there, but he said it was private. And I think he was trying to protect us; protect me in some ways.

Susan, aged 14

In their turn, some children were keen to spare their parents' feelings.

Well, my mum told me that they were getting divorced and she explained that that's like through solicitors and all that. I didn't really understand it. Like when Mum was upset, I didn't really wanna worry her with it again.

Josie, aged 13

Some children felt it would be confusing to have the legal process explained.

It's so complicated that I'm not sure if I'd understand everything that they would have said. So, really I'm not sure if I'd have liked it to be explained or not. It'd probably be explained in a certain way, and I probably wouldn't understand it.

Claire, aged 10

A few were simply uninterested.

It doesn't, it doesn't really, um, bother – well I can't think of the word now – it doesn't really bother me in any way about it. I just think that's something that someone wants to do then they can do it, can't they?

Viv, aged 14

A:   I don't really care about it.

Q:   You didn't want to have it explained to you?

A:   Na.

Jenny, aged 9

While a small number wanted to know every detail.

I think the kids should know what is going on, because I think it's very unfair to keep them in the dark. Because it's their parents. And maybe, if, when the parents are going to solicitors, maybe the solicitor or someone explaining to them [children], instead of their parents, 'cos their parents might not understand it. So, if they [children] have somebody explain what's going on, then they may find it better. But that was just my case. Other people might not want to know what's going on. That's the divorce, they don't really want to know about it. But I find it better, for me, to know what's going on, 'cos I think it's unfair to not know.

Sophie, aged 15

Indeed, as Sophie suggests, not everyone wanted to know. Just over half the children (51%) expressed interest in the legal process *per se*. Fewer still (46%) said it would have helped them to know more, or that knowing more would have altered how they felt. Thus, whilst most children appreciated that divorce was a legal process (and nearly three quarters did), they made no positive connection between knowing about it and the all-important personal, emotional and practical aspects of their parents' divorce.

I don't think I would have liked to know more but I wouldn't have really minded if I didn't know anything about it. It's more the emotional side – how other people feel about it.

Nicky, aged 12

I wouldn't like [to know] any more [about the legal process]. If I heard any more I'd probably cry.

Tim, aged 10

Q: Would you like to know about that [legal] side of things? Would you like to have that explained to you, about what goes on?

A: No. It might get me worried about what Mummy will go through.

Q: So you don't want to know about it, in case you worry about it?

A: Yeah.

Kevin, aged 12

The few children who had talked with their parents about the legal formalities of divorce, not surprisingly, had a somewhat clearer understanding of the legal process. Most of them could give broadly accurate 'legal' accounts of divorce, including the fact that their parents' marriage was not legally over until the divorce had been granted. Factual explanations of legal terms and processes helped children put some of their parents' behaviour towards each other into context.

> Divorce is like you have to go to the council thingy; well, the court, to get the divorce. But sometimes if you don't go to court and just split up, you just split up and don't see each other any more. But if you want to get divorced for total, all life, you have to go to court. You get this leaflet thing, which you have to sign. Both parents each have to sign. Fill them in. It's like a sheet thing. And they just like, get divorced. They go to leave. To go on with other people.
>
> Tim, aged 10

*A:* I think that people that are getting divorced go to see their solicitors, and they get them organised with the court. But some people don't go to court. But people who want to have custody have to go to court to fight for it.

*Q:* How do you think you'd get divorced if you don't go to the court?

*A:* I think the solicitors write letters to each other's solicitors. And then there's a paper that comes through. And they have to sign it to say.

> Lizzie, aged 12

> They separate; they have to wait a bit of time – they're still technically married then. Then they go through legal battles about nothing really. Then they ask for a divorce sheet thing, they both sign it and that's about that.
>
> Sophie, aged 14

One imagines that many parents would have had some difficulty in explaining the details of the legal process to their children, even where such an explanation might have been helpful. A few children felt that leaflets and videos might be helpful in providing them with factual information on the legal processes underway. (As we explain in Chapter 8, such leaflets have, in fact, been produced by the Lord Chancellor's Department.) However, children were quite clear that, if the legal process was to be explained, parents should be involved in the task. Children were aware of the tension implicit in this view: they acknowledged that they were reluctant to talk to their parents about the legal stages of the divorce because it was 'private' but, because it was 'private', they felt they should not be talking about it with strangers.

Q: Do you think it's important to know the legal side of things?

A: I think it is. 'Cos then you know completely what's going on, and it helps you. You know where you are, what's going on. And then, I don't think you should know every bit of it, like, 'cos some things are private to my mother. I think it should be explained to you by your parents. But I think it should only be explained to you by your parents. 'Cos then you are comfortable with who's speaking to you.

Daniel, aged 14

Direct experience of being the subjects of court proceedings, in the very small number of instances accessible to us, seemed to have very little effect on children's understanding of the legal processes. Even in these instances, children were as likely to have based their understanding on television as to have based it on their own experience.

## Discussion

As children developed an increasing awareness that their parents' marriage was coming to an end, most also became aware that their parents' were involved in divorce as a legal process. Children's knowledge of the legal process, however, was poor and the measures they took to fill the gaps (including watching television and films) frequently led them, through no fault of their own, to conclusions which were at best misleading and, at worst, wrong. Both children and their parents showed a marked reluctance to talk about the legal process. Perhaps more than in other areas we have discussed, children and parents seemed complicit in ensuring children were ill informed. It seems probable that parents found it difficult to supply the legal 'facts' in isolation because, for them (as for their children) divorce was so much more than a legal process, it was an emotional, personal and often painful experience.

The legal process was seen as a means to an end and, as such, many children (and parents) felt it was of limited importance in helping to get through the crisis of family breakdown. It may seem surprising to find that the whole panoply of the judiciary, the courts, their officers and other legal professionals played such a small part in children's accounts of their experience of divorce. The realisation that such an investment of resources by the state and its agents is marginal to most children's lived experience has profound implications, however, for how one might think of developing public policy in this area. It is to this that the next chapter turns.

## Notes

1   We should acknowledge, however, that this particular line of inquiry was pursued for our own interests in that it did not emerge as a topic of interest amongst young people during the preparatory, scooping phase of the research design. See Appendix for further details of the research design process.

2   *EastEnders* is a popular soap opera shown on the BBC.

3   *Brookside* is a popular Channel Four soap opera.

4   *Judge Judy* is a US television programme which simulates proceedings in family courts, using real families.

5   'Deirdre' is a character in the long-running ITV soap opera, *Coronation Street.*

*Chapter 8*

# *Conclusions*

## Introduction

In this last chapter, we summarise those messages from our research that might be helpful to those involved in the process of parental relationship breakdown and consider some of their implications for social policy and law reform.

As was explained in Chapter 1, our primary objective has been to present a picture of how a sample of British children between the ages of 7 and 15 viewed their parents' marriage breakdown. Two distinctive features of the study were that the children were all interviewed relatively soon after their parents' divorce and that the sample of parents was drawn from court records on a random basis representative of the divorcing population with dependent children living in England or Wales at the end of the twentieth century. As such it differs from and complements other recent British child-focused divorce studies: for example where children were the subject of court welfare reports in disputed contact or residence cases (Buchanan *et al.* 2001); where the research aim was to consider the day-to-day experience of children prevailing some three years after their parents' divorce (Smart, Neale and Wade 2001); or where the issue of parental contact was the primary focus (Trinder, Beek and Connolly 2002).

A key tenet of our approach has been to view children as social actors who observe and participate in the events associated with their parents' marriage breakdown. This reflects an increasingly significant strand of sociological and socio-legal thought concerning modern childhood. This sets out to understand children's experience in their own terms and takes the child's word as the primary source of knowledge about that experience (James, Jenks and Prout 1998). Essentially this approach is concerned with hearing the voice of the child as little mediated by professional discretion and interpretation as possible. It implies a rejection of the traditional paternalistic view of children as innocent victims of their parents' divorce to be regarded as objects of welfare rather than as young citizens who are the subject of rights and whose views need to be taken into account when decisions about their future are being taken. Our main purpose therefore as researchers has been to explore (with the consent of the children and resident parents – see Appendix) the children's views, feelings and understanding of the divorce process, and to examine their role as active participants during that process. Thus, we have endeavoured to ensure that the voices of the children, as far as possible, should come through loud and clear so as to highlight their individuality. It has not been an easy task in preparing the preceding chapters to select, from the many extensive transcripts of our interviews with the children, those extracts which both reveal and illustrate the diversity of the children's individual experience and which also reflect general themes and common experiences. Readers will have to judge how far we have succeeded in balancing these objectives. Nevertheless, looking back over the previous chapters a number of key points emerge which we consider have important implications both for parents contemplating and going through relationship breakdown and for professional practice in education, community health and social welfare as well as for social policy and law reform.

## Key research messages

### The crisis of parental separation

First, as we saw in Chapter 2, the children in our study typically experienced parental separation and the consequent upheaval in their everyday lives as a form of 'crisis'. We use the term 'crisis' here in a specific sense to mean a period of emotional turmoil and stress which temporarily disturbs normal psychological equilibrium or homeostasis (i.e. the reasonably steady state of everyday life). Typically such crises occur when people are faced with a serious threat or sudden loss (often referred to as a stressor) such as a bereavement, loss of job, onset of serious illness etc., which cannot be dealt with by the person's normal coping mechanisms (Caplan 1961, 1964, 1986, 1989; O'Hagan 1986; Rapoport 1970). As we have seen in the context of parental separation and divorce, the loss that children experience is most acutely felt in relation to the parent who moves out of the family home, but children also often fear the loss of friends and the possibility of having to leave school and familiar surroundings if there is likely to be a change of residence.

It needs to be emphasised here that in using the term 'crisis' in this sense, we are not suggesting that most children's response to their parents' separation is somehow pathological in nature. On the contrary, it is an entirely normal reaction and one that could be expected. Although what the children told us suggested, as one would expect, that their reactions to the crisis of their parents' separation varied in intensity and duration, their responses followed a familiar pattern: initial feelings of shock, disbelief or bewilderment, a degree of anxiety about the future and an intense need to recapture as much of their 'normal' lives as they could. Gradually and certainly by the time we had met them, most of the children seemed to have adapted to separation, coped with it in various ways and were back on a relatively even keel. A few however seemed 'low' or even depressed and socially isolated, particularly those who had experienced traumatic events such as domestic violence between the parents, continuing parental conflict (for example over contact arrangements) or who had suddenly lost contact with the non-resident parent.

### Children's information needs

The second major point to note is the importance to children of obtaining reliable information about the separation and divorce so that they could have a better understanding of what was happening and what to expect. Those who were well informed appeared better able to buffer the impact of the crisis and to have stronger self-esteem and a capacity to understand and manage their lives. By contrast, lack of information and confusion added to the children's uncertainties and sometimes seemed to have longer-term adverse repercussions, for example, in their relationships with their parents and any new partners. Yet, as we have seen, although we were told by almost all the parents that they had spoken to the children about their imminent or actual separation and subsequent divorce, a number of the children recalled this differently. Thus, almost a third reported not being told by either parent. As we have seen, the younger the child, the greater the chance of not being told – with only 52 per cent of those under the age of 10 being able to recall being told anything about the separation by either parent. Either children or parents may have forgotten of course but, either way, it seems to us that the issue of 'talking through' and of the child's understanding of parental separation and divorce is of crucial importance.

Parents obviously may find it difficult to raise the issue and to explain things appropriately – for example in such a way so as not to denigrate the other parent. One can readily understand such parent–child communication difficulties: separation and divorce was a new, uncharted and stressful experience for almost everyone involved. They may not have fully understood what was happening themselves and therefore did not necessarily know what to tell the children. As we have seen, children, in turn, felt that they did not know how to ask for the information that they needed. Some parents and children reported that they had shied away from talking about the divorce because each felt the need to protect the other from further worry and upset. Yet again, it is clear that some parents failed to appreciate that by not talking with their children they were compounding their children's confusion and uncertainty. Children consistently expressed the view that even though sometimes they 'could not take it all in at the time' they wanted to know what was happening as events unfolded and as their family life underwent critical change.

We realise that not all families, even those that remain intact, have adopted a 'democratic' culture of consulting children in this way. Even today there are parents who have been brought up to believe that in some respects children should be 'seen and not heard' and who think that it is out of place for children to question decisions made about them by their parents. All we can say from this particular study is that most children found it decidedly unhelpful to be kept in the dark about what was happening. As Smart and colleagues observed from their study (Smart *et al.* 2001, p.61):

> Most children want a voice in important family matters and they feel excluded and disregarded if they are denied access to any form of participation.

But the issue of 'telling' has to be handled sensitively by the parents in ways that are appropriate to the child's understanding and expanding knowledge as the life of the family unfolds. Even if they are members of the same family, each child experiences their parents' divorce uniquely. Thus parents and other relatives in seeking to give information and support to children have to learn quickly to take into account children's competence and capacity to work through and resolve the crisis at their own pace.

### Meeting the children's support needs

Not only do children need reliable information, they also need emotional comfort and support, particularly from their parents and close friends. We have illustrated in earlier chapters the various strategies and support mechanisms employed by the children in this respect. Parents were the most obvious actual and potential providers of emotional support, information and advice, with the resident parent (usually the mother) being best placed to help.

It was clear however that not all received the support from their parents that they needed. Coping with continuing conflict between the parents and divided loyalty was particularly taxing for many children. Some, especially boys, regretted the more limited access they had with their non-resident fathers. As we have seen, sometimes the children felt their parents were too upset to help or, at the other end of the scale, did not wish to be reminded of what had happened in the past because the parent had 'moved on'.

The importance of 'best friends' as sources of comfort and support cannot be overstated. Other researchers (Dunn and Deater-Deckard 2001; Smart *et al.* 2001) have also drawn attention to this. As our data show, close friends were represented as being more likely to understand, especially if they too had experienced parental divorce. Later in this chapter we explore some of the implications of children's close friendships in the context of considering ways to promote social policies and provision designed to 'support the supporters' and to improve the flow of reliable information to these vital natural peer group care-givers and first responders.

Children were more likely to be ambivalent about seeking support outside their family and circle of close friends. A few found teachers helpful and were glad they knew, not so much for the support they could offer, but more because the child hoped the teacher would better understand the cause of any deterioration in the standard of their schoolwork and behaviour. Professional support from counselling or welfare agencies such as the court welfare service or mediation did not feature significantly in our sample, although as we have seen, some had positive experience of using confidential telephone support services such as ChildLine.

Certain points emerge from the children's accounts about the way they manage intimate exchanges with people outside the family. First, children wish to control the nature of these exchanges, which, with friends, often take the form of a sharing of confidences. The children themselves manage the time, place, manner, content and language in which these communications take place. Second, such friends, particularly if they have experienced parental divorce, often seem to play an important informal role as 'passage agent', that is, as someone who can encourage, guide and support the child through all the family changes that are taking place. These special friendships seem to help the children, mobilise their own psychological resources and empower them to manage the stresses of life at home.

### Managing critical family transitions and their aftermath

The crisis of parental separation and divorce, as we have seen, is not likely to be experienced by the children as a 'one-off' event. Many had been aware of growing tensions and difficulties in their parents' relationships even though the separation itself may have come as a severe shock. For many, the aftermath of separation brought further difficulties; for example, over contact arrangements which sometimes the children were able to discuss and negotiate with parents and sometimes not. Some authors

(Clulow 1991, p.176) suggest that for both children and adults parental breakdown and separation can be harder to come to terms with and to get over than the loss of a parent through death. Moreover, Clulow observes:

> For children a sense of being to blame or of not being worth staying at home for, may affect the success of future attempts made by the departing parent to keep in touch.

Resonating with many of our own findings, Clulow further comments on the weakening of trust and confidence between child and parents that can follow the departure of the non-resident parent. He writes:

> The consequences of that can be that they (the children) worry about their future security – if one parent leaves then why not both. They may blame themselves for the rift or they become angry about their power-lessness in a situation which is not of their choosing and where their wishes and feelings appear to be disregarded by those who are supposed to care most for them. For in divorce the wishes and sometimes the inter-ests of parents and children are likely to diverge in a way that rarely happens in bereavement. (Clulow 1991, p.176)

This ongoing sense of major change and uncertainty, as we have seen, manifests itself most commonly over contact arrangements, which are often subject to a continuing degree of negotiation and renegotiation between parents and children (Trinder *et al.* 2002). At both a practical and emotional level contact has to be 'learned'. Thus we have seen how children sometimes describe the practical difficulties of having two homes, the tiresomeness of having to pack and unpack, the lack of space in their non-resident parent's (often temporary) new home; the difficulties of spending time with parents' new partners either because they do not get on with them or because they might be thought of as betraying the parent with whom they usually live.

We particularly note that in their accounts of contact arrangements, many children use the language of time as a metaphor, particularly if they lack the emotional vocabulary to describe the nature and quality of their family relationships and feelings in other ways – again an issue for boys rather more than girls. We have seen how contact could also provide opportunity for 'unfinished business' between the parents to be conducted. A number of children described having to play the role of go-between and to pass on hostile messages or to witness doorstep arguments. Others took on the role of messenger in order to prevent more explosive confrontations between their parents – another example of children taking care of stressed parents and actively engaging in the 'emotional work' of divorce. A further notable feature was the way children were concerned that contact arrangements should be seen as 'fair' to all the parties while being sufficiently flexible to allow them to maintain social relationships with friends and to continue their 'normal' recreational activities. This point about the continuity of other areas of their lives was important in helping them recover equilibrium after crisis.

However, it would be wrong to conclude this part of the chapter by summarising only the more problematic aspects of children's divorce experience. As we have seen, divorce could open up and widen children's experience of life and could bring benefits as well as disadvantages. At a practical level most of these children demonstrated to us their growing capacity to manage 'time maps' in ways and to a degree that children from intact families rarely need to. They also showed that they could often successfully manage complex and highly charged emotional relationships, sometimes on behalf of their parents. We were impressed by the capacity that many of them seemed to develop to weigh and balance competing demands – another sophisticated life skill. A number appeared to have learnt to take greater responsibility for their own lives, to take a compassionate interest in their parents and sometimes to assume responsibility for other members of the family such as siblings, even though this could be burdensome. Overall, the children in our study demonstrated a resilience and coping capacity that might surprise some. By the time we came to interview them many showed us they had reached a fairly settled understanding of the recent critical changes in their family life and were getting along positively with their own lives.

Moreover, those who had taken an active part in decisions about the arrangements and those who said they were able to talk with their parents about their problems concerning their divided lives, were more likely to have a more positive sense of their experiences. The issue therefore that we need to consider next is whether more could be done by way of community support to enable a greater proportion of children to make the best of things when their parents' relationship breaks down.

## Children and their use of social support systems: A case for a strategic public policy?

We turn now to the implications of this research for social policy and law reform. In doing so, we sketch out a simple conceptual framework upon which might be constructed new strategic thinking about how best to provide for the information and support needs of children in these circumstances. First, we need to clarify our use of the terms 'support' and 'support systems'. The approach we have adopted was summarised by Gerald Caplan some years ago (1974, p.7):

> The idea that a person receives support or is in need of support usually carries the connotation that he is weak. From this point of view the term is unfortunate because what we have in mind is not the propping up of someone who is in danger of falling down but rather the augmenting of a person's strength to facilitate his mastering of his (sic) environment... A support system implies an enduring pattern of continuous or intermittent ties that play a significant part in maintaining the psychological and physical integrity of the individual over time.

Much of what we learnt from the children about how they respond to and cope with parental divorce concerned their varying capacity to make use of available support systems – the family itself, close friends and, more occasionally, other sources such as ChildLine or professionals of one sort or another.

These social networks form an interacting complex of systems that help to sustain individuals and families as they negotiate and renegotiate their way through various key life transitions – in this instance divorce and family reconstruction. As we have seen, as far as the children are concerned, those they turned to first and most often, apart from parents and other relatives (especially grandparents), were close friends. We can term these 'first responders' because the children themselves chose them as the natural 'supporters' on these occasions.

A second line of responder, used far less often, is to be found in everyday community services with which children come into contact and in which they have confidence, including occasionally some of their teachers. Here we might also include the relatively recent development of telephone helplines such as ChildLine and internet websites such as one established by the NCH (National Children's Homes), 'It's not your fault' (www.itsnotyourfault.org.uk).

Third, there are a range of specialist back-up professional support services to be found in the health, welfare and legal field, most of which provide support to adults and, only indirectly through them, to children. But some do see children directly – for example, GPs, professionals in mental health services and practitioners from CAFCASS – the new Child and Family Court Advisory and Support Service (see below). Much more rarely, children are seen by a few family lawyers. These formal, professional services are sometimes described in community mental health terms as providing primary, secondary and tertiary preventative services. Lawyers of course are not accustomed to thinking about their services in this way even though there is evidence that their clients in part evaluate the help they receive from the perspective of how supportive the lawyer is (Davis 1988; Eekelaar, Maclean and Beinart 2000; Murch 1980).

Thus when considering social policy and law reform the key question is, 'What, if anything, can be done by way of community support to help children whose parents' relationship breaks down and as the family grapples with the associated upheavals?' This question has been phrased carefully, in part because the relevant children are not necessarily only those whose separating parents were married. The debate about the position of children in family breakdown is one about where the boundaries of the state's legitimate interest in the family lie. How far should the state's concern be taken? In a society in which a multiplicity of family forms exist, and where a substantial and increasing number of parents cohabit without being formally married, should the state's concern to promote the welfare of children be confined only to those whose parents were married and who divorced? Alternatively should the state adopt a more restrictive view that family break-up is an essentially private matter and that it is up to parents, relatives, friends and, if need be, charitable, non-governmental organisations to concern themselves with children if they so wish? This more restrictive line, of course, acknowledges that in some instances, where children are at risk of significant harm, the child protection provisions of the Children Act 1989 might need to come into play. These issues have been vigorously and extensively debated elsewhere (Bainham 1990; Barton and Douglas 1995; Cretney 1990; Douglas, Murch and Perry 1996; Law Commission 1988; Piper 1994). We do not intend to restate them here. Rather, in the light of research reported in this book and other recent studies of children's perspectives of parental breakdown, we suggest that it is time to rethink the state's traditional approach to these matters and that a new strategic social policy should be developed based on strengthening both the informal and formal care-giving systems which children and their families may access if they so wish, particularly at times of crisis.

## Developing a new strategic approach

Starting from the proposition that children need reliable information and support when faced with parental breakdown, the question is, 'How might community services be so arranged and developed to provide effective back-up to those natural care-givers and first responders which this and other studies have shown most children search out and use for themselves?' We should not forget, however, that there is also an important question: 'What, if anything, can be done for those children who have unsupportive parents and families, who are not able to find appropriate friends and who appear isolated and excluded?' As we have written elsewhere (Douglas *et al.* 2001, p.373):

> If parents are unable to provide the support they (the children) need, because of their own emotional difficulties and inability to communicate, it may be a matter of chance whether children find a suitable channel for their fears and feelings.

To provide the appropriate level of community support that we suggest is needed will require considerable development and coordination of existing resources and services and will, for reasons explained below, need to move well beyond and outside the legal system. The government itself recognised this when it produced its Consultation Paper *Supporting Families* (Home Office 1998), and subsequently established The National Family and Parenting Institute to lead the development of new services designed to help parents and children. This included the proposed expansion of the National Parenting Helpline telephone service, the development of the Sure Start scheme offering parents, in areas of greatest need, appropriate training for work, literacy and childcare; general parenting, advice and skills courses etc.; and a broader family support role for health visitors in advising and supporting parents with children over the age of 5 as well as younger children. But valuable as this major government initiative is, it still largely focuses on adult, parental support, whereas our concern is to find appropriate ways of focusing directly on children themselves. In this regard, we offer the following suggestions.

First, thought needs to be given to whether more could be done, perhaps through the educational system, to encourage, in particular, older children to develop their own 'self-help' support networks. We have in mind promoting this idea through media and television story-lines, through the setting up in schools of 'best buddy' schemes as well as through school discussion groups for children. In addition, we know again from children in this and other studies, how many children fear that teasing and bullying would result were they to reveal details about their difficulties in their private family life. Schools need to develop effective strategies to counteract this. Overall, we believe much more could be done to ensure that school itself is seen as providing a more supportive environment for children undergoing troubles at home. In these and other ways we hope that a more congenial and informed community spirit can be developed to strengthen children's capacity to deal with a whole range of major life crises – not just those arising from family breakdown.

A second line of approach is to bring these and related research messages more to the attention of practitioners working in the complex of services which seek to address parental tensions and conflict – not just counsellors in the marriage guidance field but particularly family doctors and those concerned with child health and welfare. Here we have in mind that a number of children told us that they would have liked more whole family discussions when decisions about their future were being negotiated. This of course raises complex issues about the desirability of promoting the democratisation of family life since not all families accept the value of parent–child discussions of this kind. More fundamentally, in terms of facilitating family support services, it brings the whole idea of listening to and accommodating the voice of the child into long-established professional discourses.

It seems doubtful whether any welfare professional's working week passes without some reference to 'participation' or 'engaging the user'. (It is a racing certainty that 'partnership' is mentioned on a daily basis.) Yet, where such partnership involves children, much, we would argue, remains paternalistic and largely adult-focused (Douglas *et al.* 2000; Lowe and Murch 2001; Lyon, Surrey and Timms 1998; Roberts 1998; Scanlan, Perry and Robinson 2000). There remain many practitioners who will need to undergo a shift of mindset if they are to develop the necessary skills and understanding to see children as key social actors with valid views of their own which need to be understood and responded to in their own terms. This will require a major investment in well-designed programmes of continuing professional education in health, legal and social services. As far as those working within the family justice system are concerned, as Lowe and Murch pointed out (2001, p.157), now that the President of the Family Division has established an Interdisciplinary Committee with a special education and training sub-committee, the opportunity exists to review all the core competencies of family justice practitioners including their skill levels in working with children (i.e. judges, solicitors, barristers and staff of the new CAFCASS). If, as is expected, the Lord Chancellor approves the creation of a National Family Justice Council with its own education and training committee following the Consultation Paper issued in March 2002 by his department, and if the necessary funding is provided, then a concerted effort to bring professional training into line with the modern participant approach to children might become a reality.

We would stress however that our findings imply more than the acquisition of new skills on the part of certain professionals. If the actual experience of divorce for children is to be factored into any professional response we might make, the children in this study have indicated some important areas for us to reflect upon: we might need to recognise children's own pace and sense of 'balance' in the timing of formal proceedings; we might have to recognise the difficulty that children have in expressing their emotions and be sensitive to their use of metaphor and alternative forms of expressing emotion, such as crying; we would need to recognise the real importance of a child's friends and to take these into account as much as any other factor when the post-divorce arrangements are being brokered and we would need to differentiate between children who each experience their parents' divorce uniquely, even if they are members of the same family, for example. We would also have to take into account children's competence in resolving the crisis themselves and the part they play in managing the crisis for others.

The third area of community support concerns the legal world – the family justice system which regulates the exit from marriage through divorce (itself in effect a licence to remarry) and which deals with child-related disputes either through the promotion of settlement by negotiation and mediation or by way of adjudication. We explained in Chapter 1 how, partly under the influence of international conventions such as Article 12 of the United Nations Convention on the Rights of the Child 1989, ratified by the United Kingdom in 1992, and of the Human Rights Act 1998 which brought the main provisions of the European Convention into domestic law, there has been a growing recognition of the idea of children's rights and of listening to the voice of the child in administrative and legal proceedings concerning them. Moreover, in other fields of family law, such as adoption and child protection, courts for a number of years have had a statutory duty to ascertain the wishes and feelings of children subject to their maturity and level of understanding. But this does not yet apply, except in limited fashion, in the realm of private divorce law. So, what more can be done to make this branch of the law compliant with the requirements of international law and the increasingly dominant view concerning the participation of children?

As we also explained in Chapter 1, since the 1940s, there has been a growing recognition and concern about the position of children in divorce. Had the provisions of the Family Law Act 1996 been implemented, courts would have been required when dealing with the divorce petition, to first have regard to a 'checklist' of factors which would have included ascertaining the 'wishes and feelings of the child, considered in the light of his age and understanding and the circumstances in which those wishes were expressed'. This would have been in line with the expressed duty of that Act to treat the welfare of the child as paramount.

Even though the legislation was not brought into force, the lessons of the pilot schemes that tested out its key features were drawn on by government to introduce procedural and practice reforms. The pilots showed a desire by those undergoing divorce for more information and individual advice at different stages of the divorce process and for help of different kinds. They also showed how difficult parents found it to discuss frankly and helpfully with their children critical issues arising from the marriage breakdown and how these might be tackled by the family as a whole (Walker 2001). Accordingly, the Lord Chancellor's Department commissioned the design of four information leaflets directed at both adults and children in different age groups, to be circulated to all solicitors and freely available over the internet. It is hard to judge how effective this approach will be, but the signs are not encouraging as far as distribution via solicitors is concerned (Douglas and Murch 2002). The government also decided to trial a scheme of Family Advice and Information Networks (FAINs) (Legal Services Commission 2001) aimed at improving the amount of information available to parents. This experimental scheme recognises the key role that solicitors play as 'gatekeepers' to the system of divorce and the strategic position they might be in to encourage their clients to use other family support services, including mediation. To date, we have no idea how effective this scheme is going to be. The Legal Services Commission is committed to carrying out research to evaluate it, including a proposed specialist study of the provision of direct services to children.

But perhaps the most fundamental development to occur following the failure to implement the divorce reforms was the establishment, in 2001, of a new service, the Children and Family Court Advisory and Support Service (CAFCASS), under the Criminal Justice and Court Services Act 2000. This brought together three separate services, all concerned with providing support and advice to courts dealing with family proceedings. The court welfare service operated as the civil wing of the probation service, providing an investigative and reporting facility to courts dealing with private family law matters (arising, for example, on divorce or between unmarried couples in dispute over their children's futures) and offering mediation to the parties to help them settle their disputes (Buchanan *et al.* 2001). The *guardian ad litem* service provided representation for children who were the subjects of public law proceedings; *guardians* would themselves instruct lawyers who would provide legal representation of the child in court. The Official Solicitor acted as a *guardian ad litem* for children in private law disputes where the court considered that there was a conflict of interest between the parents in dispute and the child.

It will be seen that all three services were essentially concerned with ensuring that what was in the child's best interests could be ascertained and presented to the court to enable the judge or magistrates to reach the appropriate decision in the case and enabling the court to obtain guidance beyond the partisan advocacy presented by the adult parties themselves. As the name of the new service implies, it was not envisaged as simply having an investigative or advocacy role. Family support, utilising the services experience and skill in direct face-to-face work with children, was also intended as a key function. Therefore, CAFCASS' terms of reference are wide. They are to safeguard and promote the welfare of children; to give advice to any court about any application made to it in family proceedings; to make provision for children to be represented in such proceedings; and to provide information, advice and other support for children and their families. One can see here further attempts to ensure that families and children receive a broad information and advice service when caught up in family disputes. Unfortunately, the organisational problems experienced in bringing these three services together and workload pressures have meant that up to the end of 2002, the service has struggled simply to maintain its statutory responsibilities to provide welfare reports for the courts.

The Lord Chancellor's Department is also giving further thought to the value and use of parents' statement of arrangements concerning children required under the provisions of Section 41 of the Matrimonial Causes Act 1973. A number of researchers over the years have shown that, at least as a child welfare check, this procedure is of little more than symbolic value (Davis *et al.* 1983; Douglas *et al.* 2000; Elston, Fuller and

Murch 1975; Murch *et al.* 1999). Nevertheless, there have been sugg-estions that it could be converted into a form of Parenting Plan, which might, in appropriate instances, include reference to the views of children. The idea of a Parenting Plan came originally from Australia. In effect, the plan is a checklist of matters that it is suggested separating parents need to take into account when making arrangements for their children. As the preamble states, it is 'designed to help you (i.e. the parents) make arrange-ments for your children and to discuss these with them and others who may be involved'. The Plan is a voluntary exercise, not an enforceable contract of any kind, and it may have to be altered from time to time in the light of changing circumstances. Thus, the procedure might become a tool to help parents focus their thoughts on the future of their children rather than a strict legal requirement with possible sanctions for non-compliance.

Public concern about domestic violence and its impact on children, highlighted by the Children Act Sub-Committee of the Lord Chancellor's Advisory Board on Family Law, and by parliamentary questions, has also prompted a response from the Lord Chancellor's Department aimed at ensuring that contact arrangements made in such cases are 'safe' as far as the children are concerned (Lord Chancellor's Department 2002b, 2002c). Thus far, the government has limited its response to this area of concern to encouraging the development of a family communication and information strategy through the National Family and Parenting Institute and CAFCASS; promoting the use of Parenting Plans through the voluntary sector; and monitoring the development of the FAINs initiative. Furthermore it has increased its grant to various child contact centres, making £1.5million available in the period 2000 to 2002 for the development of training materials aimed at promoting increased vigilance in cases where there is considered to be a high risk of violence.

Just as this book was about to go to press, the Cabinet Office issued a press release (30 October 2002) (CAB 091/02) (www.gnn.gov.uk) reporting that the Prime Minister had announced the government's intention in the New Year to issue a Green Paper for consultation concerning 'children at risk'. It was stated that this would consider measures to:

Reduce levels of educational under-achievement, offending, anti-social behaviour, teenage pregnancy and ill health.

It was further stated that:

The Green Paper will focus on the identification, referral and tracking of children at risk and the provision of mainstream and specialist services for them. It will look at an overhaul of existing arrangements and at services working with children and young people including social services, youth justice, as well as the roles of schools, families and communities.

Commenting on the announcement, Paul Boateng, the Chief Secretary to the Treasury, is reported in the press release as saying:

This Green Paper is about ensuring that we prevent children and young people dropping out of education, committing crime and suffering from family conflict and ill health. Investment in schools, health, social services and the criminal justice system has to be matched with reforming services and ensuring they are organised around the needs of children and young people.

From the point of view of practical politics and as a way of securing extra resources, it is understandable if strategic government thinking in the United Kingdom should seek to address the needs of children with separating and divorcing parents within a broader conceptual framework primarily concerned with preventing various harms to children – educational under-achievement, teenage pregnancy, anti-social behaviour etc., sometimes viewed as the symptoms of family breakdown and divorce. In this context, the statement of the Minister for Children and Young People, John Denham, made at the time the Prime Minister announced the Green Paper, might be particularly significant. The Minister said:

Prevention has been at the heart of the Government's approach to tackling social exclusion… We have to go further. Too many children are only given the help they need when they reach a crisis point. We are asking local authorities and other agencies to have preventive strategies in place across England next year and local authorities are taking work forward on the identification, referral and tracking element of this in order to provide targeted services for those children most at risk. The

Green Paper will enable us to look at the whole scope of children at risk to ensure we tackle the problems as early as possible.

But this is not an approach we would wish to endorse as far as children with separating parents are concerned. We dislike the possible stigmatising element of labelling children as being at risk of developing delinquency, anti-social behaviour etc. Rather we take a more positive view that the state could do more to ensure that a greater degree of information and community support is available to its young citizens in these circumstances as of right as well as with the aim of reducing their social exclusion and stress when decisions affecting their future are being made. The approach that appeals to us most is that adopted by the Irish government's National Children's Strategy (2000, p.10) in its comprehensive review of children's services within the Irish Republic. This strategy wholeheartedly endorses the participant approach to children who are:

> respected as young citizens with a valued contribution to make and a voice of their own; where all children are cherished and supported by the family and the wider society and where they enjoy a fulfilling childhood and realise their potential.

Not only would such a vision and approach be more in line with the principles of the United Nations Convention on the Rights of the Child 1989 to which the United Kingdom is a signatory, but also, as has been argued elsewhere (Douglas *et al.* 1996), one way forward in pursuit of such an objective would be to utilise more fully the provisions of Section 17 of the Children Act 1989, criticised in the past by Sir William Utting for its hitherto, too restrictive application (Utting 1995). Section 17 imposes a duty upon local authorities to safeguard and promote the welfare of 'children in need in their area' by providing a range of parenting support services. It is certainly possible to argue that this research has made a convincing case that many children are at least temporarily 'in need' and that resources should be directed at finding out the most appropriate ways of identifying and reaching the children concerned and of providing those crisis support services likely to be most acceptable to parents and children alike.

## Pointers to the future

All these initiatives might be considered laudable but we take the view that many of them are *ad hoc*, uncoordinated and reflect an ambivalent uncertain stance as far as the participation of children is concerned. Moreover, up to now it has not been clear whether there is any coherent strategic thinking going on across all relevant government departments, although the announcement of the forthcoming Green Paper on children at risk may herald a change of approach. We suspect there are a number of reasons why in the past things have been developed piecemeal. First, there is the question of principle to be resolved – does the state have a responsibility to the children in these circumstances or not? If it does, what should be its extent? Second, there is the major problem of scale to be dealt with. We are here talking about a critical life-changing event that affects tens, even hundreds of thousands of children every year. This is bound to raise concerns about the cost to the public purse. Nevertheless we take the view that it should be possible to develop a coherent strategic approach, not necessarily at any greater public expense than exists at the moment, based on an analysis of community support systems such as we have sketched out above.

As far as resolving the issue of principle is concerned, we think there is abundant evidence to show that it is both desirable and possible to consult children, even as young as 5 years old, when decisions are being made about their future. Moreover, the principle of children's participation in administrative and legal decision-making is enshrined in international and domestic law. So, the problem now is more to do with overcoming the persistence of traditional adult mindsets that exclude children and translating principles into practice.

As for the question of scale, on the face of it this is a formidable obstacle in developing any social provision other than on a token basis. Moreover, to be added to the 'official statistics' is the large (but difficult to estimate precisely) number of children whose *unmarried* parents separate. But already, in a number of ways, the community costs of meeting the needs of all these children must be high. For example the level of demand for court reports prepared by CAFCASS in private law cases is running at about 3000 a month and from the six-month period from 1 October 2001 to 31 March 2002 some 17,352 reports for the courts were received (CAFCASS 2002). It would be possible to make further calculations of cost such as the demand on court time and the expense to the legal aid fund to say nothing of other potential support services in the educational, health and welfare fields.

We would suggest that the question of expense needs to be approached by asking whether the existing costs are falling in the right places, at the right time and in the most appropriate ways. If more was devoted to reinforcing front-line responders (for example, through various schemes in schools, youth groups and through media programmes and the like) then more might be saved later on by avoiding the need to investigate and support families and children once they have become involved in disputes about contact and residence. This is because, as we have seen, the legal machinery only comes into the picture after formal court proceedings have commenced, and often long after the crisis of separation when the needs of children and parents for support and information are most acute. If their needs are not appropriately met when the main crisis is upon them, then unhelpful parental attitudes and conflicts can escalate, become entrenched and compounded. Moreover, it should not be forgotten that moments of crisis properly handled can be moments of opportunity for growth and positive thinking. So why do we not plan our support systems on that basis?

Finally, we should emphasise that what we are advocating is the development of information and support services that children and their parents can access voluntarily if they so wish at a time of their own choosing. We are not talking about imposing more paternalistic welfare intervention but rather primarily strengthening those natural care-giving networks which children and families already use. More specialist back-up support services need to be developed only where children and their parents cannot, for one reason or another, use their normal network of front-line responders. As far as the risk of serious harm to children is concerned, the existing provisions under the Children Act 1989 should be adequate if court orders are needed. Nor are we suggesting that this approach to support services should be confined only to those children whose parents were previously married and divorced. There is no child welfare or community mental health reason to differentiate children in this way. In so far as this strategic thinking needs to consider the work of the family justice system in informing and supporting children in these circumstances it needs to be approached within the framework of a family law focused primarily on parenthood and children's interests rather than marriage and divorce. To guarantee to children their appropriate voice in these matters that so closely affect them, to give children's perspectives and understandings of the divorce process the respect these deserve, it will be necessary to ensure that knowledge about the role children can play in helping our understanding of family change becomes embedded in public knowledge and public norms and opinions about the value of children.

It is our contention that the position of children in their parents' divorce, both in formal, professional and in familial contexts can be more usefully understood if it starts from a recognition that it is we (as adult professionals or simply as professional adults) who need to find our place in a complex personal and social dynamic in which children are already active participants rather than they who need to mesh with systems, practices and procedures that are designed to meet ends more allied to our particular interests and habits of thought. Children know what they think of their experience and can point to ways in which we, as adults, might help them deal with their experiences. They are the best witnesses to that experience and we, as adults, have as much to gain from our involvement with them as they have from their involvement with us. As one young person put it:

Q: Is there anything that could be done, that would help you? By other people? Or...?

A: Probably, if more people understood what it was like to go through divorce, and if they knew what it was like to experience how bad it was.

Q: What sort of people would need to know?

A: Probably more children would need to know. More adults would have to understand children's feelings; others have to understand what children feel. Not what they feel, but what the children feel about it.

Q: Do you think any adults do understand what children feel?

*A:* Some of them do, but a lot think, well, they have feelings, but they don't care that much about it, because they're only kids, they don't like care but a lot of children do suffer from it and they just don't know what to do. They're like me! They don't know what to do. *(Laughs)*

*Appendix*

# How to Listen to Children

Exploring the sensitive, often painful subject of family breakdown directly with children, and doing so shortly after their parents' divorce had been finalised, presented us with a number of ethical and methodological challenges. In this appendix we describe how we met these challenges through the careful design and development of our research method, procedure and tools. As many of the challenges we faced – how to talk to children, how to help children feel secure and in control, the question of informed consent – are not exclusive to research or researchers, this appendix is likely to be of interest and use to a wide range of people who work with children.

## Overview

Our key research aim was to explore with children their first-hand experience of living through parental separation and recent divorce. Our research design allowed us to work with a random, representative sample of families, to talk to children relatively soon after their parents' divorce had been completed (on average within 15 months (standard deviation two months) of *decree nisi* being granted), and to collect quantitative data from children, resident parents and court records to complement our qualitative interview data. These features contributed to the rigour and empirical strength of our study and made it distinctive from other contemporary studies examining children and divorce.

For the quantitative data, it is important to stress that these were not intended or used to interpret or qualify children's accounts. Instead, they serve to complement the children's spoken word, to compare the child's and parent's views on certain issues, to present a profile of the children and adults who took part and to enable us to relate our findings to a more general population.

## Securing a sample

### Random court sample

Our first challenge was to secure a random, representative sample of recently divorced parents. To help with this, we sought permission from the Lord Chancellor's Department to draw a sample from court records. This sampling strategy gave us access to a representative population that other strategies (e.g. advertising in the press, workplace or support group noticeboards, word of mouth) would not have afforded.

We took a number of steps to try to ensure a representative sample. We drew cases from six courts across South West England and South Wales (Bristol, Exeter, Yeovil, Cardiff, Newport, Swansea) which, taken together, gave a demographic and geographic mix of city, town and country. The number of cases drawn from each court was proportionate to that court's caseload. This calculation was based on the number of petitions made and *decree nisi* granted by the court between 1994 and 1996 (Lord Chancellor's Department 1996; Office for National Statistics 1997). We included contentious and non-contention cases, and cases regardless of the child's relationship to the divorcing adults (e.g. birth parents, step-parent and birth parent).

We drew our sample during August and September 1997. To ensure the children we subsequently interviewed had recently experienced their parents' divorce, we drew our sample from lists showing all cases granted *decree nisi* between January and August 1997 (interviews were conducted in 1998). Court service staff supplied these lists of pronouncements. From each list, we drew a random sample, retaining cases which had an address for (at least) the resident parent and included at least one child between 8 and 14 years of age. Each case retained was given a unique reference number to protect confidentiality.

From court records, we collected information on the cases retained including number, date of birth and sex of children involved; whether mother or father was the resident parent; details on the marriage and divorce (e.g. date of marriage, and *decree nisi*, 'grounds' for divorce petition); and any special circumstances (e.g. child with a disability, orders for residence or contact, injunctions for violence). Indications of violence were noted to help reduce risk to parents or children (see below) and to help us consider the researchers' safety when making home visits to interview the children.

With the agreement of court service managers, we prepared a letter to be sent to both divorcing adults in the cases retained. In a few cases, no letter was sent to the non-resident parent either because of indications of violence on the part of that person against another family member or because no address was held. The letter sent explained the role of the Lord Chancellor's Department and court services in the research, introduced the research itself and invited parents to consider taking part. It included a contact number for further information and gave a closing date for return (freepost) of the 'opt out' reply slip. It was made clear that opting out would not influence ongoing legal proceedings. The letter was sent through, and replies returned to, the court services. At the time of drawing the sample, we compiled lists showing the name, address, court number and unique reference number of each person to whom a letter had been sent. This list was left with court service staff to allow them to delete details of those opting out. Deletions were readily made by matching the reference number shown on both the list and reply slip. The amended lists were collected from court services on a pre-arranged date. In essence, these sampling procedures were designed to protect the confidentiality of those who opted out of the study, for the research team at no time held names or addresses of these people.

Of the 315 cases drawn from court records, 73 per cent (that is of resident parents) did not opt out, 24 per cent did opt out and 3 per cent of letters were returned by the Post Office as 'not known at this address'. Initially, we intended to secure the consent of both parents before involving children in the study. However, of the resident parents not opting out, 40 per cent of their former spouses (i.e. non-resident parents) in these cases either opted out (22%) or could not be traced (18%). This raised practical and ethical issues. First, securing the consent of both parents would have reduced the sample and increased the likelihood of it being unrepresentative. Second, it would have prevented a large number of resident parents and children deciding for themselves whether or not to take part. This seemed unreasonable and so we decided to proceed by securing the consent of resident parents only.

### Recruiting gate-keeping parents

The next step was to contact the resident parents (229) who had not opted out. We did this by sending a newsletter (December 1997). The challenge here was to ensure that gate-keeping parents felt adequately informed about the research and sufficiently confident in us to allow us to approach their children. The newsletter format lent itself to this for a number of reasons. Through it we were able to provide clear information on the research, its purpose and possible value in some detail; to write about what would be involved in taking part; to address concerns parents might have about involving their children (e.g. causing unnecessary upset) and, partly by suggesting that parents show the newsletter to their children, to stress the centrality of children to the research. The newsletter format also provided the opportunity to begin to build a rapport with families by including a photograph of the researchers who would conduct the interviews, by giving biographical details stressing their suitability for conducting sensitive research with children and by supplying contact details (freepost, e-mail, telephone number). Another strength of the newsletter was that it might be seen as less threatening, and to some degree less personal, than a letter on University stationery. We felt this less formal approach might prompt a more favourable response and reduce any irritation or annoyance parents might feel at us contacting them directly. A freepost postcard was enclosed with the newsletter. Parents were asked to return it saying whether or not they were interested in taking part in the study. By the closing date, 18 per cent of families had replied agreeing to take part, 6 per cent had opted out and 2 per cent of newsletters were returned by the Post Office as 'not known at this address'.

In early January, parents who had not replied to the newsletter and for whom a telephone number could be traced (using Directory Enquiries and BT's online database) were contacted by telephone. This secured a further 11 per cent positive and 9 per cent negative responses. It is worth noting that none of the people contacted in this way, essentially 'cold called', objected. No one expressed displeasure or anger that their personal details and family circumstances had been released to us. Most people said they had forgotten or 'not got round to' replying, others said that they simply had not bothered to reply. These responses suggest that an 'opt out', as opposed to 'opt in', policy for recruiting research samples might not be the ethical minefield it may sometimes be thought to be. Used selectively and with care, it can be an effective means (as it was for us) of securing a representative study sample.

Our target was to interview 100 children. To help us reach this target, in March 1998, the remaining non-respondents (54%) to the first newsletter were sent a personal letter inviting them to take part. Key points made in the first newsletter were repeated. With this letter, we enclosed a copy of our second newsletter. This newsletter, which had already been sent out to those families who had agreed to join the study, provided a progress update and made reference to the number of families who had already agreed to take part. This contact resulted in a further 5 per cent positive and 5 per cent negative responses and 1 per cent 'not known at this address'. In August, this process was repeated for the remaining non-responders (then 43%), this time enclosing our third newsletter.

## Parents' reasons for opting out and opting in

We persisted with recruitment because we wanted a representative sample. At each point of contact, additional families took up or refused our invitation to take part so it proved worthwhile recruiting over an extended period of time. Indeed, a number of parents explained that their decision was influenced by the stage they felt they or their children had reached when we made contact with them. A few said they only felt able to make a 'balanced' decision some time after our initial contact. Reflecting this, a parent who did not opt out until August 1998 wrote:

> I have thought about this [taking part], but feel my son has suffered enough as it is. We want to put the whole sorry mess behind us and get on with our lives.

Although parents were not asked why they had opted out, 20 volunteered a reason. Seven simply said they did not want their children involved. Others explained that:

> They [the children] are doing really well. I don't want to add to the pressure.

> He [the children's father] left two years ago. The children are only just beginning to settle.

> His [the child's] behaviour was affected by the divorce, I don't want him involved.

One more surprising response was:

> The children don't know [about the divorce].

A smaller number of parents provided reasons that were much more to do with how they felt themselves rather than how their children might be feeling:

> I just want to put it behind me.

A number of parents who were interested in taking part also gave reasons for their decision. Some said they felt their children might benefit from having someone listen to their side of the story. To this a few added that they had been unable themselves to do this for their children whilst in the throes of the divorce. Particularly in the latter instances, we stressed (as we did to all families) that we were not offering professional help or counselling, indeed quite the reverse; we were seeking families' help to investigate what it was like for children to live through their parents' divorce. Many children found the idea that they were helping us, and through us possibly helping other children and adults, very appealing. In a few cases, this idea swayed their decisions in favour of taking part.

## Recruiting children

When parents agreed to take part, they were contacted again, usually by telephone, to discuss the research further, for the researcher to try to ascertain the child's willingness to participate and to make a provisional appointment for a named researcher to visit the family to interview the child. (All families opted for home visits rather than to meet at the researchers' university or some other suitable location.) With the parent's permission, the child was sent a personal letter by the named researcher who would, if the child agreed, conduct the interview. This letter was written in a language children might readily understand. It was printed on specifically designed, rather than university, stationery to make it more accessible and child-friendly. In the letter, we stressed points already made in our newsletters to help ensure children were able to make an informed decision about taking part. In particular, we stressed that it was for the child to decide whether to take part in the interviews and that he or she could opt out at any time without repercussions. None of the children contacted opted out and the provisional appointments made with parents were confirmed in a letter sent to the child.

## Our representative sample

We put considerable effort into tracing and retaining families from the initial random court sample to try and ensure a representative sample of children participated in the study. At the end of the recruitment process, of the initial court sample, 30 per cent of families (93) had opted in, 36 per cent (113) had opted out, 30 per cent (93) had not replied (we have no way of knowing if they received our letters) and 5 per cent (16) could not be traced. Thirteen parents who would not agree to their children taking part nonetheless said they would be willing to take part themselves.

Of the 93 families who opted in, 23 were subsequently lost to the study. Despite measures to keep in touch with all interested families (e.g. sending regular newsletter updates), when we came to make appointments nine could not be traced. In another case the parents were reconciled and again living together. Eleven more families 'withdrew' by various means including being out when the researcher visited (one family), cancelling appointments at the last minute (five families) or simply declining to make an appointment when contacted (five families). In another case, contact with the child had been made through his mother, however, when the researcher called, the child's father answered the door and refused her access saying his ex-wife had not told him about her visit. Where appropriate we tried to reschedule visits but, in all cases, without success. In most of these instances, we do not know if the decision to withdraw was adult or child-driven. In the remaining case, it was certainly the child's decision. Here, despite his father's protestation and inducements, the child closed his bedroom door and refused the researcher admittance. The researcher accepted this readily and made to leave. However, she did not manage this for some 30 more minutes. The father, who wanted to talk about his own situation, suggested she wait, as he was sure his son 'would come round'. He was clearly less willing to accept that the child's word was final.

Our final sample comprised 70 families (65 mother-headed households, five father-headed households). From these families, we interviewed 104 children (51 girls and 53 boys) – 38 single children, 30 pairs of siblings and two sets of three siblings. All children chose to be interviewed without other family members present. At the time of the interview, on average (standard deviation), children were 11 years and 6 months old (26 months), their parents had been legally divorced (*decree nisi*) for 15 months (2 months) and separated for 3 years 1 month (19 months).[1]

Analysis of data collected from court records shows that these 70 cases and 104 children were representative of the initial random court sample across key variables including number of children in divorce petitions, children's age and gender, relationship of children to divorcing adults (e.g. birth parent, step-parent), length of marriage, parents' civil status at time of the marriage, 'grounds' (i.e. fact relied upon in the petition), court where petition was filed and whether legal aid was granted. On this evidence, we were satisfied that we had achieved a random, representative sample of children and parents with recent experience of divorce.

*Parent's questionnaire*

When we visited families to interview children, we also asked the resident parent to complete a questionnaire. This questionnaire was designed to collect quantitative information on the divorce, family demographics and standardised measures on parental behaviour (e.g. well-being, social support), child behaviour (e.g. problem behaviours) and parent–child relationships. Some of the same questions and measures were completed by children and so provided directly comparable information. Parents were asked to complete the questionnaire either during the visit or to return it in the freepost addressed envelope provided. Sixty-six parents (96%) completed the questionnaire. It was explained at the start of the visit that within two weeks of the Parent Questionnaire being returned, the family would be sent a cheque for £30 as a 'thank you' for taking part. To help with this, parents completed a form giving the exact name to be shown on the cheque and the address to which it should be sent. These forms also served as a record for budgeting purposes. Children knew about the honorarium and in many cases they were to be given all or a share of the money, at the parent's discretion.

## Communicating with children

The challenge of communicating effectively with children was central to all aspects of our research design. Indeed, our study depended on our ability to meet this challenge.

There is evidence to suggest that adults and children often speak in different 'dialects' and that neither is wholly confident or fluent in the other's version of English (Butler and Williamson 1994). It tends to be the case that when adults (including adult professionals) talk to children, they assume – if they think about it at all – that the child will adapt to the adult's register, idiom and tone. This, however, seriously disadvantages the child and considerably limits the value and effectiveness of the exchange for both parties. We wanted to reverse these expectations in order to reduce or remove the related disadvantages and limitations experienced by children. We wanted to help children talk freely to us in their own way and using their own words. We wanted to enable children, regardless of age or ability, to feel comfortable talking to us – strangers and professional adults. Importantly, we wanted children to feel in control of what was happening. We wanted to create conditions that would allow us to understand, and to be understood by, the children whose social worlds we were interested to explore. With these objectives in mind, we put considerable thought into the design of our procedures and tools.

## KIDs name and logo

To help children identify with the research we devised a logo that would appeal to them and a name that they would feel comfortable using. The logo was selected from a standard graphics software package. The name was changed from 'children's experience and perceptions of the divorce process' to the KIDs Project (KIDs was an acronym for Kids In Divorce). The name and logo were used on the materials we designed and feedback indicated that both appealed to children across the study age range.

## KIDs newsletters

Throughout the life of the study, we wrote regular newsletter updates. In the early stages newsletters were used to help recruit families to the study. Our rationale for selecting a newsletter format was that it allowed us to design attractive, eye-catching communications that we could make accessible, interesting and informative for a wide range of ages and abilities. The format was flexible enough to incorporate simple, clear language, 'headlines' and different typefaces to emphasise points and to include photographs and graphics. In addition, it lent itself to being printed on coloured paper that added to the overall visual impact. For recruitment purposes, newsletters were sent to resident parents, but at all other times they were sent to the children themselves. In families where siblings took part, each child received his or her own copy of the newsletter. The newsletters proved a useful, popular and effective means of keeping in touch with the children.

## KIDs website and e-mail

We felt it was important to use modern forms of communication since increasingly children are able to access them. Given this, we set up a dedicated e-mail address (kids@cardiff.ac.uk) and designed our own website (www.cardiff.ac.uk/claws/kids). E-mail did not prove popular possibly because, at the time (between 1997 and 2000), few of the children had ready access to it. Our website, however, was very popular, recording many 'hits' each month. We know that many of the children visited it and that a number of them showed it to friends. It also stimulated wide interest, encouraging a range of people to contact us.

Our website was launched early in 1998. Initially it contained information on our aims and objectives and photographs and biographical details on the research team. As the study progressed, the website evolved to become a more attractive, interesting, child-friendly medium. Later versions included comments, views and quotations from the children, progress updates and details of presentations we had given which helped highlight the research's applied value. (The idea of helping others through the research was important to many of the children.) The final version of our website reported key findings illustrated by quotations from children. We believe that one of the reasons our website was so successful was that it was updated regularly during the life of the study, so was always worth revisiting.

*Practical aids to communication*

At all points of contact, we invited children to get in touch and always supplied reminders of our freepost and e-mail addresses and telephone number to help them do so. We let children know when our website was updated (e.g. through newsletters). We sent them specially designed KIDs Christmas cards. As well as these practical devices, we designed tools to use during our visits to help establish, maintain and aid effective communication between the children and ourselves. The KIDs Activity Book played a key role in this (see below).

*Consent form*

Throughout our contact with families, we stressed that it was the child, not just the parent, who had the choice of agreeing to take part in the study. We also made it clear that we guaranteed confidentiality and would not disclose any information of any sort, other than through the publications we hoped the research would generate. In this form, all information would be suitably anonymised. We explained that non-disclosure meant that nothing the child told us would be disclosed to the parent (or anyone else) without the child's express permission but that the child was free to talk about the interview if he or she chose.

This particular position we took in relation to the disclosure of information will be uncomfortable for many and, we fully accept, is open to question. Our position was informed by two major considerations. First, children have reported (Butler and Williamson 1994) that the 'loss of control' over information (even of a highly sensitive nature which may indicate that a child is at risk) may lead to consequences that are more harmful (in the child's judgement) than the circumstances described by the child. This can be especially the case where the response made by welfare professionals is either precipitate or inadequate. Second, we take the view that children are rendered safer, both individually and generically, if they are empowered to make decisions, including those relating to the disclosure of information, in such a way that they retain their confidence in adults who will respect the child's agency. Children will disclose more freely to those in whom they have confidence and whom they can rely upon to do what they say. The only exception to our general position is in the case of immediate and substantial danger to life and limb.

Additionally, we carried helpline and support group information (e.g. ChildLine) to give to children, if necessary. Happily, it was never necessary either to disclose information or to pass on helpline information.

To try to ensure these conditions were understood and were 'shared knowledge', at the beginning of each visit the researcher sat down with the child and parent together to go over them. The consent form was designed to facilitate this process. After talking about the conditions and their implications, the child and parent were asked to sign the consent form. We hoped that signing would encourage, particularly parents, to accept and abide by the conditions; the researcher also signed the consent form to show she too agreed to abide by the conditions. Beginning each visit in this way was also designed to give the researcher an opportunity to assess the child's willingness to participate, to reinforce the child's status as key participant and to help provide the child with some sense of being in control of the research process. At the end of this process, the child was asked, in front of the parent, whether he or she wanted anyone else present during the interview. Most children had already decided and all chose to be interviewed on their own, out of sight and sound of other people.

### Activity book: Introducing the research, building a rapport, and helping children feel in control

Each child was given his or her own copy of the KIDs Activity Book at the beginning of the research process (i.e. the time the researcher and child spent alone together). The activity book was then used at various points throughout the meeting. The activity book was designed to serve three main purposes. First, to introduce and explain the research process to the child. Second, to help build a rapport between the child and researcher and help the child feel comfortable and in control. Third, to enable us to collect qualitative and quantitative data from the child. Our rationale for choosing the activity book format was that it enabled us to design a tool that met these purposes by engaging children in interesting and fun activities. The format was also sufficiently flexible to enable us to accommodate different ages and abilities. In addition, children were familiar with the format (e.g. through school workbooks). The KIDs Activity Book was written in language children either could read for themselves or could read with the help of the researcher. It would not have been possible to write to suit all possible reading ages. Throughout, the activity book was peopled with characters (again using graphics software) and included devices (games, drawing space etc.) to add light relief and offer children diversions and opportunities to rest. Such components could be adapted or dropped to suit the age, ability and interests of the child taking part.

The first purpose of the activity book was to help the researcher talk to the child about the research, what would happen and what could be expected during their meeting. The cover page had space for the child's name and unique reference number. This allowed the researcher to explain how data could be kept whilst ensuring individual anonymity. This, in turn, could be linked to the issue of confidentiality already raised in newsletters, letters and by the consent form. The cover page also had space for the researcher's name. This allowed the researcher to repeat her name and get the child accustomed to and relaxed about using it. This was important because the researcher, to all intents and purposes, was an unknown adult; the child might feel unsure how to address her or might feel awkward calling her by her first name. Additionally, the cover page incorporated the University and research funder's (Economic and Social Research Council) logos along with the study's name and logo. These elements offered the opportunity to provide the child with more general information about the research.

The first and second pages of the activity book listed a number of important points that could then be discussed to help the child feel relaxed and in control. The first page emphasised that we were interested in the child's own views and feelings; that there were no right and wrong answers; that the child could stop at any time without explanation or repercussions; that the researcher would work with the child and provide information or help at any time. In a few of the sentences, there was a blank space where the researcher's name could be filled in (e.g. _____ will help you). This was designed to give the child practice and to help her or him feel at ease using the researcher's first name. The second page focused on the fact that the child was not obliged to answer questions the researcher asked. This was an important point to make because children generally expect (and are expected) to do what adults say. Refusing to answer might, in practice, have been rather difficult for some children. To help with this, the second page included a game designed to help children say 'no' and to help the researcher demonstrate that there would be no repercussions for refusing to answer. The game comprised a list of straight-forward questions (e.g. 'What's your name?' 'What age are you?' 'Do you have a brother?'). The child was invited to select a question or questions that he or she would refuse to answer when asked. To help further, the child and researcher talked about different way of saying 'no' (e.g. 'I don't want to answer', 'Pass', 'Can we move on to the next question please?').

The activity book next moved on to a warm-up activity that the child could complete with ease. As well as a warm-up, this activity served several other purposes: it enabled the researcher and child to develop their rapport further; it provided the researcher with background information to draw on during the interview; it allowed the researcher to make a gentle transition between the warm-up and the interview itself. The warm-up activity was a family mapping exercise. Through the activity book, we explained that we wanted to know a little about the important people in the child's life (described as, 'The people you know, care about, spend time with, talk to, go to if you have a problem'). Space was provided either to write a list of these people or to 'draw' a family map; most children chose the latter. The page provided for the drawing was blank apart from a simple border. Using the coloured stickers we provided, the child placed a sticker on the map to represent each important person, then marked the sticker with the person's initials or name. To help the child complete the activity book we gave each one a packet of pens at the outset (they were given to them at the end of our meeting as a 'thank you').

The two methods used for completing the warm-up were selected because they allowed the activity to be completed within a relatively short time (10 to 20 minutes) and offered children of different ages and abilities a choice. A few children opted to draw people rather than use stickers. This sometimes gave the researcher the additional task of ensuring that the child did not spend too much time making a detailed drawing of each person. From the family map the researcher next moved on to interview the child by asking, for example, why the child thought 'Mummy and Daddy didn't live together anymore'.

*Interviewing children*

We decided, as far as possible, to conduct interviews during school holidays. We made this decision because it allowed us to visit children during the day rather than after they had returned from a busy day at school or at weekends when many of them wanted to spend time with their non-resident parents. Visiting during the day allowed children to fit us in around their other activities and allowed us to take a more leisurely pace over the interview so avoiding children (and researchers) becoming too tired. We completed 64 per cent (67) of interviews during the summer holidays and 21 per cent (22) during the autumn half-term holiday; interviews not conducted during school holidays were conducted in the early evening. We started interviewing in June and finished in November 1998. June, however, was not a good time because it clashed with that year's football World Cup. We quickly abandoned the idea of June interviews because we knew we would be unable to equal the excitement of live football matches!

The interview was conducted using a semi-structured interview schedule. The schedule was developed from pilot work, including in-depth interviews with five young people (aged 17 to 25) who had experienced parental divorce as children, two focus groups of school pupils (aged 12 to 13), some of whom had personal experience of family breakdown, and four children selected at random from our initial court sample. The schedule covered those themes/areas that pilot groups had identified as important (e.g. finding out, forming new, post-divorce relationships with parents). We also included legal aspects of divorce as we were interested in the child's point of view and understanding of this area in particular. We chose a semi-structured schedule because it provided a common set of topics, questions, cues and prompts. These helped the researcher to follow the child's train of thought and contribute to the ongoing flow of conversation. The semi-structured format left children free to raise issues they felt were important and to do so in the order that they chose. The schedule was designed as the researcher's *aide memoire* rather than as a tool to dictate, structure or restrict the child's words or chosen direction.

All of the children opted to be interviewed on their own by the researcher, many in their own bedrooms. Before the visit we requested 'somewhere quiet' to conduct the interview but, other than that, the location was left to the family. We found that most families had discussed the location beforehand and, in the majority of cases, children themselves seemed to have decided on their own bedrooms. Neither parents nor children found this an odd location. Children seemed to feel it was quite normal to take their guest to the privacy of their bedrooms. That, indeed, we were accepted in this way suggests our earlier attempts (e.g. newsletters, letters) to build up a rapport were successful. The child's bedroom was an ideal location to help create our preferred interview conditions for it was the child's own private space, somewhere he or she felt relaxed, comfortable and in control. Where children had clearly elected to be interviewed on their own but parents had suggested a less private location (e.g. kitchen, living room, even in a few cases, hallway), the researcher made every effort to ensure the child could talk openly without being overheard (e.g. by closing the doors).

When child and researcher were settled, the researcher asked the child's permission to tape-record their conversation. She explained that, with the child's permission, the tape-recording would be transcribed to help her remember accurately what the child had said. All children agreed to being recorded. During the interview (and at all other points during the visit), the researcher stopped if she judged the child was bored, tired or becoming distressed. Although this happened in a few cases (less than 5%), it did not result in any interviews being totally abandoned. Children, including those who became distressed, were keen to keep going. For most children, we offered an outlet that had not previously been available to them. We provided a neutral person who was interested, willing to listen and who would not act on what the child said. Our guarantees of confidentiality and non-disclosure were very important in helping children see us in this light.

### Activity book: How to make filling in questions fun

When the interview ended and the child was ready to continue, the final section of the activity book was completed. These pages comprised eight measures focusing on divorce-related issues and standardised measures (e.g. self-esteem, child–parent relationships). The challenge here was to design this section in such a way that it would hold the children's attention. This was not an easy task given the type of activity and range of ages and abilities of the children taking part. We took a number of steps to meet this challenge.

Each measure had the same pattern of pages: an opening page, followed by an instruction page, then pages with the measure itself and finally a 'rest and assess' page. Each type of page was a different colour and this, along with the pattern of pages, was designed to help the child control the process by giving him or her some idea of what was coming next and how far it was to the end. The 'rest and assess' pages were designed to provide opportunities for the child to take a break, draw, play a game, change the subject or simply to stop altogether. They also enabled the researcher to assess whether the child was too tired or bored to continue. Just as characters (i.e. taken from graphics software) were used elsewhere, here each measure had its own character. Where the researcher judged it appropriate, the character was used to introduce the measure, support and encourage the child whilst completing the measure (e.g. the character might crop up saying, 'Keep going, you're doing well') or to help assess the child's ability or willingness to continue (at the end of a measure the character might say, 'Are you sure you want to go on?'). The researcher also adapted the 'rest and assess' pages to suit the child completing the activity book. In this section, and throughout the activity book, we were careful to place pages to ensure that information on related points could be seen without turning pages, for example in this final section we were careful to place instruction pages facing the questions they were describing to allow for ready reference between the two.

Overall, the activity book served its stated purposes well. Although the research process lasted between 90 and 180 minutes, with the majority of children taking about 120 minutes to complete both the activity book and the interview, only four children failed to complete everything. Of these, three completed all but a few pages of the activity book. The other child, who had shown limited interest in the interview, decided to watch television rather than do any of the final section of the activity book. Despite the length of our visit and the tasks involved, we invariably found it was the children who urged the researchers on, saying that they were quite able to go on and wanted to complete the whole activity book.

*Ending the visit*

For most children, we had been talking about difficult, upsetting matters so we took steps to ensure that all children were left on a positive note. Each session ended with the researcher asking the child to reflect on their experience, to say what were the worst and best points, what they thought they had learned or gained, and what advice they would give to other children, parents and adults who might have to deal with divorce in the future. By acknowledging their expertise through these questions, we helped to reinforce the child's feeling of self-worth and were able to ensure that no child was left upset or distressed. Before leaving, the researcher presented the child with his or her own personalised KIDs Certificate. Most children were thoroughly delighted with this and a number insisted the researcher wait while the certificate was put up on their bedroom wall or placed in a folder with their other prized possessions.

## Children's views on taking part

It is still a commonly held adult view that children should not be involved in painful or sensitive matters – a view which certainly extends to involving children in research (e.g. Smart *et al.* 2001). However, through the careful design and development of our research we have shown that children can and want to be involved in matters which affect them and, moreover, that they are interested and willing to contribute to research which accurately documents their views and experience.

Towards the end of the research, in June 2000, some 20 to 24 months after we had conducted the interviews, we contacted the children again. We invited them to tell us how they were getting on and what it was like to take part in the KIDs Project. Nearly 40 per cent (40) of them replied (a further 5% of letters were returned as 'not known at this address'). From their replies, we found that most children were glad that they had taken part, and they frequently stressed the importance they attached to the research's potential to help others. (The ages shown after these quotations are those of the children in June 2000.)

> The good thing about helping was that I knew it would go towards research for children in a similar position as me.
>
> Sean, aged 16

> I thought it was a good idea so children could let other people know how they felt.
>
> Charlie, aged 13

> I enjoyed working with KIDs because it was a chance to help others with their experiences of divorce and convey what divorce is like from a child's point of view to adults.
>
> Oliver, aged 15

> It felt really good to talk to KIDs 'cos it felt like I was doing something to help. I was glad to do it.
>
> Sophie, aged 17

Added to their sense of having helped others, a number of children found taking part personally beneficial.

It was good to take part in the KIDs Project because it helped me realise what I really felt about my situation. It was also good to think I was helping someone else.

Libby, aged 15

A good thing about taking part was that we could get stress in our minds out in the open.

Tony, aged 12

Other children were pleased to have had someone to listen.

It felt good because I could talk to people and express my feelings.

Ollie, aged 11

It gave me a chance to tell someone what I felt like.

Samantha, aged 15

I specially liked when I said how I felt when my mum and dad split up.

Joe, aged 10

We believed that our design and the development of method, procedure and tools combined with our attitude towards children, enabled us to engage with them and helped them talk to us. Many children agreed:

The good thing about taking part is that it was fun.

Gillian, aged 11

It was fun, I enjoyed it a lot and I would like to do it again sometime.

Stephen, aged 12

I found the KIDs Project interesting and informative.

Shaun, aged 14

Most children enjoyed taking part and a considerable number made positive comment about the activity book.

I liked it when I filled in the papers.

Joe, aged 10

It was easy to answer the questions.

Oscar, aged 14

I enjoyed colouring the pictures.

Kate, aged 11

The children appreciated the efforts we had made to create conditions that enabled them to talk freely about a difficult, and for many still painful, experience. This included our guarantees of confidentiality and non-disclosure of information and, very importantly, our willingness to listen without judging.

I was very happy to take part in the KIDs Project. I was happy to tell my problems to someone I trust.

George, aged 12

I was a bit upset because it brought back the divorce but after the interview, I was happy that I shared my problem with someone.

Sioned, aged 14

It was good to get my feelings out without people to stop me. But it also reminded me of the non-stop arguments and the tears.

Abby, aged 13

It brought up a lot of feelings but I enjoyed taking part because it was nice to be able to talk to someone about my parents' divorce.

Nicky, aged 14

The rich body of data we gathered has helped us demonstrate that children want to be and can be involved in matters which affect them and that they can talk in a considered, insightful and articulate way about sensitive, personal issues. Through this explanation of how we went about gathering our data, we hope we have demonstrated that, with preparation and careful thought, adults can engage in meaningful dialogue with children about difficult subjects.

## Note

1    Standard deviation is a commonly used measure of dispersion (or spread). The more widely the scores are spread out, the larger the standard deviation.

# References

Achenbach, T. M. (1991) *Manual for the Child Behavior Checklist / 4–18 and 1991 Profile*. Burlington, VT: University of Vermont, Department of Psychiatry.

Allison, P. and Furstenberg, F. F. Jr. (1989) 'How marital dissolution affects children: Variations by age and sex.' *Developmental Psychology 25*, 540–549.

Archard, D. (1993) *Children, Rights and Childhood*. London: Routledge.

Archard, D. (2001) 'Philosophical perspectives on childhood.' In J. Fionda (ed) *Legal Concepts of Childhood*. Oxford: Hart Publishing.

Aries, P. (1960) *L'Enfant et la Vie Familiale sous L'Ancien Regime*. Paris: Libraire Plon. Translated by R. Baldick (1962) *Centuries of Childhood*. London: Jonathan Cape.

Bainham, A. (1990) 'The privatisation of the public interest in children.' *Modern Law Review 52*, 2, 206–221.

Barton, C. and Douglas, G. (1995) *Law and Parenthood*. Butterworths: London.

Beck, U. and Beck-Gernsheim, E. (1995) *The Normal Chaos of Love*. Cambridge: Polity Press.

Best, J. (ed.) (1989) *Images of Issues: Typifying Contemporary Social Problems*. New York: Aldine de Gruyter.

Block, J., Block, J. H. and Gjerde, P. F. (1989) 'Parental functioning and the home environment in families of divorce: Prospective concurrent analyses.' *Annual Progress in Child Psychiatry and Child Development*, 192–207.

Brown, J. and Day Sclater, S. (1999) 'Divorce: A psychodynamic perspective.' In S. Day Sclater and C. Piper (eds) *Undercurrents of Divorce*. Aldershot: Ashgate.

Buchanan, A., Hunt, J., Bretherton, H. and Bream, V. (2001) *Families in Conflict – The Perspectives of Children and Parents on the Family Court Welfare Service*. Bristol: Policy Press.

Butler, I. (1996) 'Safe? Involving children in child protection.' In I. Butler and I. Shaw (eds) *A Case of Neglect? Children's Experiences and the Sociology of Childhood*. Aldershot: Avebury.

Butler, I. and Pugh, R. (2003) 'The politics of social work research.' In R. Lovelock, K. Lyons and J. Powell (eds) *Reflecting on Social Work*. Aldershot: Ashgate.

Butler, I. and Williamson, H. (1994) *Children Speak: Children, Trauma and Social Work*. London: Longman.

CAFCASS (2002) *Annual Report and Accounts 2001 – 2002 HC1208*. London: The Stationery Office.

Caplan, G. (1961) *An Approach to Community Mental Health.* London: Tavistock Press.

Caplan, G. (1964) *Principles of Preventive Psychiatry.* London: Tavistock Press.

Caplan, G. (1974) *Support Systems and Community Mental Health – Lectures in Concept Development.* New York: Behavioural Publications.

Caplan, G. (1986) 'Recent developments in crisis intervention in the promotion of support systems.' In M. Kessler and S. E. Goldston (eds) *A Decade of Progress in Primary Prevention.* Hanover: University Press of New England.

Caplan, G. (1989) 'Prevention of psychopathology and maladjustment in children of divorce.' In M. Brambring, F. Losel and H. Skowronek (eds) *Children at Risk: Assessment, Longitudinal Research and Intervention.* Berlin: Walter de Gruyter.

Clulow, C. (1991) 'Making and breaking and remaking marriage.' In D. Clark (ed) *Marriage, Domestic Life and Social Change: Writings for Jackie Burgoyne. (1944–1988).* London: Routledge.

Cockett, M. and Tripp, J. (1994) *The Exeter Family Study: Family Breakdown and its Impact on Children.* Exeter: Exeter University Press.

Collier, R. (1995) *Masculinity, Law and the Family.* London: Routledge.

Coulshed, V. (1991) *Social Work Practice: An Introduction.* Basingstoke: Macmillan Educational.

Cretney, S. (1990) 'Privatising the family: The reform of child law.' *Denning Law Journal,* 15–26.

Davis, G. (1988) *Partisans and Mediators.* Oxford: Clarendon Press.

Davis, G., Macleod, A. and Murch, M. (1983) 'Undefended divorce: Should Section 41 of the Matrimonial Causes Act 1973 be repealed?' *Modern Law Review 46,* 2, 121–146.

Davis, G. and Pearce, J. (1998) 'Privatising the family?' *Family Law,* 614–617.

Davis, G. and Pearce, J. (1999) 'On the trail of the welfare principle.' *Family Law,* 144–148.

de Mause, L. (1976) *The History of Childhood.* London: Souvenir Press.

Demo, D. H. and Acock, A. C. (1988) 'The impact of divorce on children.' *Journal of Marriage and the Family 50,* 619–648.

Douglas, G. and Murch, M. (2002) 'Taking account of children's needs in divorce – a study of family solicitors' responses to new policy and practice initiatives.' *Child and Family Law Quarterly 14,* 1, 57–75.

Douglas, G., Murch, M. and Perry, A. (1996) 'Supporting children when parents separate – a neglected family justice or mental health issue.' *Child and Family Law Quarterly 8,* 2, 121.

Douglas, G., Murch, M., Robinson, M., Scanlan, L. and Butler, I. (2001) 'Children's perspectives and experience of the divorce process.' *Family Law 31,* 373–377.

Douglas, G., Murch, M., Scanlan, L. and Perry, A. (2000) 'Safeguarding children's welfare in non-contentious divorce: Towards a new conception of the legal process.' *Modern Law Review 63*, 177.

Dunn, J. and Deater-Deckard, K. (2001) *Children's Views of their Changing Families.* London: Joseph Rowntree Foundation/YPS.

Eekelaar, J. (1986) 'The emergence of children's rights.' *Oxford Journal of Legal Studies 6*, 2, 161–182.

Eekelaar, J., Maclean, M. and Beinart, J. (2000) *Family Lawyers – The Divorce Work of Solicitors.* Oxford: Hart Publishing.

Elston, E., Fuller, J. and Murch, M. (1975) 'Judicial hearings of undefended divorce petitions.' *Modern Law Review 38*, 6, 609–640.

Fortin, J. (1998) *Children's Rights and the Developing Law.* London: Butterworths.

Fortin, J. (1999) 'The HRA's impact on litigation involving children and their families.' *Child and Family Law Quarterly 11*, 3, 237–255.

Freeman, M. (1983) *The Rights and Wrongs of Children.* London: Frances Pinter.

Giddens, A. (1991) *Modernity and Self-Identity.* Cambridge: Polity Press.

Giddens, A. (1992) *The Transformation of Intimacy.* Cambridge: Polity Press.

Gould, N. (2000) 'Qualitative research and the development of best attainable knowledge in social work.' *Theorising Social Work* (www.nisw.org.tswr/gould/html).

Hammersley, M. (1992) *What's Wrong with Ethnography?* London: Routledge.

Harter, S. (1985) *Manual for the Self-Perception Profile for Children.* Denver, CO: University of Colorado.

Herring, J. (1999) 'The Human Rights Act and the welfare principle in family law – conflicting or complementary?' *Child and Family Law Quarterly 11*, 3, 223–236.

Hetherington, E. M. (1989) 'Coping with family transitions: Winners, losers and survivors.' *Child Development 60*, 1–14.

Hetherington, E. M., Cox, M. and Cox, R. (1985) 'Long-term effects of divorce and remarriage on the adjustment of children.' *Journal of the American Academy of Child Psychiatry 24*, 518–530.

Hetherington, E. M. and Stanley-Hagan, M. (1999) 'The adjustment of children with divorced parents: A risk and resiliency perspective.' *Journal of Child Psychology and Psychiatry 30*, 1, 129–140.

Home Office (1998) *Supporting Families.* London: The Stationery Office.

James, A. L. and James, A. (1999). 'Pump up the volume: Listening to children in separation and divorce.' *Childhood 6*, 2, 189–206.

James, A., Jenks, C. and Prout, A. (1998) *Theorising Childhood.* Polity Press: Cambridge.

James, A. and Prout, A. (eds) (1997) *Constructing and Reconstructing Childhood: Contemporary Issues in the Sociological Study of Childhood* (Second Edition). London: Falmer Press.

James, A. and Richards, M. (1999) 'Sociological perspectives, family policy, family law and children: Adult thinking and sociological tinkering.' *Journal of Social Welfare and Family Law 21*, 1, 23–39.

Jessop, J. (1999) 'The psychology of divorce: A review of the literature.' In S. Day Sclater (1999) *Divorce: A Psychosocial Study*. Ashgate: Aldershot.

John, M. (1996) 'Voicing: Research and practice with the "silenced".' In M. John (ed) *Children in Charge: The Child's Right to a Fair Hearing*. London: Jessica Kingsley Publishers.

Kelly, J. (1993) 'Current research on children's post-divorce adjustment.' *Family and Conciliation Courts Review 31*, 29–49.

Key, E. (1900) *Barnets Århundrade(The Century of the Child)*. 1909 New York and London.

King, M. and Piper, C. (1995) *How the Law Thinks about Children* (Second Edition). Aldershot: Arena.

Kovacs, M. (1981) 'Rating scales to assess depression in school aged children.' *Acta Paedopsychiatry 46*, 305–315.

Law Commission (1988) (Law Com No 172). *Guardianship and Custody*. London: HMSO.

Law Commission (1990) (Law Com No 192) *The Ground for Divorce*. London: HMSO.

Lee, N. (2001) *Childhood and Society: Growing Up in an Age of Uncertainty*. Buckingham: Open University Press.

Legal Services Commission (2001) *Family Advice and Information Networks – Consultation Paper*. London: Legal Services Commission.

Lord Chancellor's Department (1996) *Judicial Statistics Annual Report (1996) England and Wales for the year 1995*. London: HMSO (CM3290).

Lord Chancellor's Department (2002a) *Judicial Statistics: England and Wales for the Year 2001*. London: The Stationery Office.

Lord Chancellor's Department (2002b) *Increasing Safe Contact for Children and Their Families*. Conference Report. London: Lord Chancellor's Department.

Lord Chancellor's Department (2002c) *The Government's Response to the Children Act Sub-Committee Report 'Making Contact Work'*. London: Lord Chancellor's Department.

Lowe, N. and Murch, M. (2001) 'Children's participation in the family justice system – translating principles into practice.' *Child and Family Law Quarterly 13*, 2, 137–158.

Lyon, C. M., Surrey, E. and Timms, J. E. (1998) *Effective Support Services for Children and Young People When Parental Relationships Break Down: A Child-Centred Approach*. Liverpool: Centre for the Study of the Child, the Family and the Law (Liverpool University Press).

MacCormick, N. (1976) 'Children's rights: a test-case for theories of right.' *Archiv fur Rechts und Sozialphilosophie 62*, 305–317.

MacFarlane, A. (1986) *Marriage and Love in England: Modes of Reproduction.* Oxford: Blackwell.

Mitchell, A. (1985) *Children in the Middle.* London: Tavistock.

Moore, M., Sixsmith, J. and Knowles, K. (1996) *Children's Reflections on Family Life.* Cambridge: Polity Press.

Murch, M. (1980) *Justice and Welfare in Divorce.* London: Sweet and Maxwell.

Murch, M., Douglas, G., Scanlan, L., Perry, A. and Lisles, C. (1999) *Safeguarding Children's Welfare in Uncontentious Divorce: A Study of s 41 of the Matrimonial Causes Act 1973.* Research Series 7/99. London: Lord Chancellor's Department.

National Children's Strategy (2000) *Our Children – Their Lives.* Dublin: The Stationery Office.

Office for National Statistics (1997) *1994 Marriage and Divorce Statistics for England and Wales* (FM2 No.22). London: HMSO.

Office for National Statistics (2002) *Social Trends 32.* London: The Stationery Office.

O'Hagan, K. (1986) *Crisis Intervention in Social Services.* London: MacMillan.

O'Halloran, K. (1999) *The Welfare of the Child: The Principle and the Law.* Aldershot: Ashgate Arena.

Opromolla, A. (2001) 'Children's rights under Articles 3 and 8 of the European Convention: Recent case law.' *European Law Review 2001, 26 Supp (Human Rights),* 42–56.

Owen, D. (1995) *Nietzsche, Politics and Modernity.* London: Sage.

Perry, A., Douglas, G., Murch, M., Bader, K. and Borkowski, M. (2000) *How Parents Cope Financially on Marriage Breakdown.* London and York: Family Policy Studies Centre and Joseph Rowntree Foundation.

Piper, C. (1994) 'Looking to the future for children.' *Journal of Child Law 6,* 3, 98–104.

Piper, C. (1996) 'Divorce reform and the image of the child.' *Journal of Law and Society 23,* 3, 364–382.

Pollock, L. H. (1983) *Forgotten Children: Parent–Child Relations from 1500 to 1900.* Cambridge: Cambridge University Press.

Quartrup, J. (1994) 'Recent developments in research and thinking on childhood.' Paper at XXXI International Sociological Association Committee on Family Research. London: April 1994.

Rapoport, L. (1970) 'Crisis intervention as a brief mode of treatment.' In R. W. Roberts and R. H. Nee (eds) *Theories of Social Casework.* Chicago: The University of Chicago Press.

Reece, H. (1996) 'The paramountcy principle – consensus or construct?' *Current Legal Problems 49,* 267–304.

Roberts, M. (1998) 'Children and the mediation process.' In *UK College of Family Mediators, Directory and Handbook 1998/99.* London: Sweet and Maxwell.

Rodgers, B. and Pryor, J. (1998) *Divorce and Separation: The Outcomes for Children.* York: Joseph Rowntree Foundation.

Scanlan, L., Perry, A. and Robinson, M. (2000) 'Listening to children in divorce: The gap between principle and practice.' *Representing Children 13*, 1, 34–47.

Seltzer, J. A. (1991) 'Relationships between fathers and children who live apart: The father's role after separation.' *Journal of Marriage and The Family 53*, 79–101.

Shaw, I. (1996) 'Unbroken voices; children, young people and qualitative methods.' In I. Butler and I. Shaw (eds) *A Case of Neglect? Children's Experiences and the Sociology of Childhood.* Aldershot: Avebury.

Shorter, E. (1976) *The Making of the Modern Family.* London: Collins.

Smart, C. and Neale, B. (1999) *Family Fragments?* Cambridge: Polity Press.

Smart, C., Neale, B. and Wade, A. (2001) *The Changing Experience of Childhood: Families and Divorce.* Cambridge: Polity Press.

Smith, B. H. (1997) *Belief and Resistance: Dynamics of Contemporary Intellectual Controversy.* Cambridge, Massachusetts: Harvard University Press.

Stone, L. (1977) *The Family, Sex and Marriage in England 1500–1800.* London: Weidenfeld and Nicholson.

Thompson, N. (2000) 'Crisis intervention.' In M. Davies (ed) *The Encyclopaedia of Social Work.* Oxford: Blackwell.

Trinder, L., Beek, M. and Connolly, J. (2002) *Making Contact: How Parents and Children Negotiate and Experience Contact after Divorce.* York: York Publishing Services.

Utting, W. (1995) *Family and Parenthood: Supporting Families and Parenting Breakdown.* York: Joseph Rowntree Foundation.

Van Bueren, G. (1995) *The International Law on the Rights of the Child.* Dordrecht and London: Martinus Nijhoff Publishers.

Van Bueren, G. (1996) 'The quiet revolution: Children's rights in international law.' In M. John (ed) *Children in Charge: The Child's Right to a Fair Hearing.* London: Jessica Kingsley Publishers.

Walker, J. (2001) *Information Meetings and Associated Provisions within the Family Law Act 1996 – Key Findings from the Research.* London: Lord Chancellor's Department.

Wallerstein, J. S. and Kelly, J. B. (1980) *Surviving the Break-Up: How Children and Parents Cope with Divorce.* New York: Basic Books.

# Subject Index

# Author Index